Part One

# Odyssey of Grace

## *The New Testament in Review, from Matthew to Galatians*

Cy Mersereau

ODYSSEY OF GRACE: PART I



Printed in Canada

ISBN: 978-1-4866-0000-7
eBook ISBN: 978-1-4866-0001-4

Word Alive Press
119 De Baets Street Winnipeg, MB R2J 3R9
www.wordalivepress.ca

WORD ALIVE
PRESS

FSC
www.fsc.org
MIX
Paper from responsible sources
FSC® C016245

Cataloguing in Publication information can be obtained from Library and Archives Canada.

Bethany Erin Mersereau
Born: August 15, 1982, London, Ontario, Canada
Died: May 3, 2015, Smithsburg, Maryland, United States
Daughter of Dana and Bonnie Mersereau
Niece of Cy Mersereau
A beneficiary of God's grace.

*For by grace you have been saved through faith, and that not of yourselves; it is the gift of God, not of works, lest anyone should boast.* (Ephesians 2:8–9, NKJV)

# Acknowledgments

I gratefully acknowledge all those individuals who have undergirded me with their prayers, encouragements, and helpful suggestions. Special thanks to Bonnie Carter, who has patiently and steadfastly brought this first part of *Odyssey of Grace* to its completion. Her diligence is especially noted in the massive revamping of the Gospel of Matthew, as well as her meticulous handling of the conclusion which is largely occupied with the testimony of C.S. Lewis. She has also studiously tracked down research material and continues to handle all the correspondence with Word Alive Press.

Thank you, too, for all the wonderful people at Word Alive Press. Their editing skills and expertise have been invaluable in giving the reading public what we hope will be a greater appreciation for the New Testament.

# Contents

**This first volume of *Odyssey of Grace* consists of the first nine books** of the New Testament beginning with the Gospel of Matthew and concluding with the book of Galatians. The second volume, a separate publication, covers the last eighteen books of the New Testament from Ephesians to the book of Revelation. This introductory material refers to both volumes of *Odyssey of Grace*.

In these volumes, each of the twenty-seven books of the New Testament are outlined and summarized. Special attention is given to the four Gospels, the book of Acts, and Revelation. More material is devoted to the book of Revelation then any of the other twenty-six books.

# Word from the Author

I am pleased you have obtained a copy of this book. The New Testament is a divinely inspired document far beyond the capacity of any book, including this one, to adequately flesh out. The special sections indicated by the symbol ♛ are meant to heighten your interest and enhance your understanding of the intricacies of the New Testament Scriptures. Better still is the hope that you will feel encouraged to give much more time and attention to reading and studying the words of Holy Writ. This book is punctuated by a number of these special sections that point to passages and topics that mandate more detailed attention.

I haven't hesitated to enter into passages and topics that are difficult or controversial. Some are persuaded that Christ suffered in hell for a time following His crucifixion. We shall look at the fallacies of this persuasion. The timing of the suicide of Judas should also make for a lively discussion. You may be surprised to learn that the traditional teaching on this subject isn't necessarily supported by the Scriptures.

Additionally, a perusal of various commentaries will reveal that the early goings of Philippians 2 have been the subject of ongoing controversy that strikes a nerve with some. I refer to the so-called "emptying out" passage. The story of the two sons in Luke 15 makes for a fascinating study. This riveting account tells of two wayward sons, not one.

The three days and three nights of Jonah in Matthew 12:40 have prompted endless discussion since they were first penned by the tax collector turned disciple. At first glance, this verse seems not to square with other Gospel accounts.

In this book, the sometimes contentious issue of speaking in tongues is not avoided. Not all will agree with my assessment. I also discuss the matter of physical healing.

The Kingdom Now movement is an extreme element I have found difficult to ignore. Many sincere Christians are identified with this more radical form of Christianity. This influential faction is bent on the restoration of apostles and prophets in our time, and they preach an agenda for permanent physical healing and the raising of the dead. These subjects are deserving of careful examination.

You will find no prophecy chart within these pages. Some study Bibles tend to reinforce an already settled conviction and confine all other views to the sidelines. Bible commentaries do much the same.

Some aspects of prophetical truth are not without difficulty and controversy. I have strong reservations about an unbending insistence that a single position is the only legitimate one when equally sincere Christians come to other conclusions. Revelation 19:10 tells us that *"the testimony of Jesus is the spirit of prophecy"* (NKJV). This verse clarifies what the odyssey of grace is all about. There is no greater opportunity for Christians to exemplify love for each other than in those areas where we may differ. Galatians 6:2 says that we are to shoulder each other's burdens, thus exhibiting mutual love. It's easy to love those with whom we are in full agreement, but quite another to bear with those with whom we differ.

Christians who disagree on matters of lesser importance should exercise due restraint and resist the temptation to employ anger and argumentation to make their point. Our supreme example of a gracious spirit is the Lord Jesus, who endured the opposition of sinners and even gave His life for them (Hebrews 12:1–3). This attitude is further emphasized in Philippians 2:5, where we are admonished to adopt the mind of Christ in our relationships with others.

It is not imperative that we have a ready answer for every minute detail of prophetical utterance. A dogmatic assertion that we must all agree on every jot and tittle is asking for the unreasonable and impossible.

The gathered individuals in Acts 1:6–7 who were curious about the timing of future events were deftly waved off by the Lord Jesus. He reminded them that they would soon be empowered by the Holy Spirit with soul-winning power (Acts 1:8). As He ascended to heaven, the onlookers were informed that this same Jesus would return in the same manner as they then witnessed (Acts 1:9–11).

It is imperative that we remain focused on the Lord Jesus as well as the task at hand, which is winning souls to Him. The Lord Jesus Christ is the very essence of Scripture and the more time we spend in its sacred pages, the more familiar we become with He who *"is called The Word of God"* (Revelation 19:13, NKJV).

# Preface

*For the law was given by Moses, but grace and truth came by Jesus Christ. No man hath seen God at any time, the only begotten Son, which is in the bosom of the Father, he hath declared him.* (John 1:17–18, KJV)

The story is told of a mythical Greek king who returned home following a victorious campaign at the city of Troy. The harrowing ten-year voyage is vividly described by a poor blind epic poet whose name was Homer.[1] This lively tale is loaded with romance, fearful creatures, and high adventure featuring sea nymphs (sirens), a one-eyed mutant, and a sorceress called Circe.[2] The Trojan horse used as a ploy to deceive and defeat the stubborn army of Troy is credited to Odysseus, or Ulysses to the Romans.[3] In his honour, the poem is called *The Odyssey*. In today's

[1] Una McGovern, ed., Chambers Biographical Dictionary (Edinburgh, UK: Chambers Harrap Publishers, 1997), 745.

[2] Robert Graves, *The Siege and Fall of Troy* (London, UK: The Folio Society, 2005), 95–99.

[3] Ibid., 74–75.

English vernacular, an odyssey indicates any adventurous journey or an intellectual or spiritual quest.

The Lord Jesus ventured from His home in heaven to initiate His odyssey of grace over two thousand years ago. His odyssey began in a stable of Bethlehem, and it ended on a Roman cross more than thirty-three years later. Many of those who witnessed His death felt they had seen the last of the Nazarene, but three days later He arose bodily from the grave in resurrection power.

The Scriptures tell us that grace and truth came by Jesus Christ. He has declared the Father. The Greek word for declare is *exegeomai*, from which we derive the word exegesis. This simply means that Christ explained and interpreted the nature of God when He became one of us and lived among us for a brief period of time (John 1:17–18).

The true story of the Lord Jesus is unlike the largely fictional tale of Odysseus and his companions as they returned to the Greek Isle of Ithaca. While Odysseus lived in a culture of no morality, code, or law, the Lord Jesus fulfilled the perfect law of God, meeting all of its demands and sealing the New Covenant with His precious blood. The Greek warriors worshipped numerous gods while our Saviour's odyssey of grace made it possible for us to have a personal relationship with the one true God.[4]

The Lord Jesus Christ is the central figure of the New Testament, the books of which represent the second major division of the Bible. He is the driving force of the entire document. He is named in the first verse of the first chapter of the first book (Matthew 1:1) and appears in the last verse of the last chapter of the last book (Revelation 22:21). His blessed influence is felt throughout like an effervescent and pungent perfume emanating from its heavenly source.

The New Testament, or New Covenant, is clearly distinct from the Older Testament, but it must not be severed from it. One writer has said,

---

[4] *Encyclopedia Britannica, Volume 16* (Chicago, IL: William Benton, 1962), 711–712; for the Homeric poems, see: *Encyclopedia Britannica, Volume 11* (Chicago, IL: William Benton, 1962), 699–703.

"The OT presents itself then as a story that is headed somewhere."[5] The same writer continues the same thought regarding the New Testament:

> The NT authors, most of whom were Jewish Christians saw themselves as heirs of the OT story, and as authorized to describe its proper completion in the death and resurrection of Jesus and the messianic era this ushered in.[6]

## THE BIG STORY

The story in both testaments leads ultimately to the Big Story, the Lord Jesus. His odyssey of grace is the heart and soul of the New Testament Scriptures.

The Old Testament was far more than a simple agreement between God and Israel, but rather "an intimate relationship based on loyal love."[7] The defining moment for Israel, and for the entire Old Testament, was the giving of the law on Mount Sinai. *The Holman Illustrated Bible Dictionary* says that "the Mosaic Covenant was brought about not by an act of conquest but by God's gracious deliverance of Israel from bondage.[8]

The law given through Moses "is presented as an object of delight and admiration"[9] (Psalm 1:2; 119:16, 47, 77). Contrary to how the law is often seen from our vantage point,

> the law is never presented in the OT as a list of rules that one must obey in order to be right with God; rather it is God's fatherly instruction given to shape the people He has loved and saved into a community of faith, holiness, and love, bound together by mutual support and care.[10]

---

[5] *ESV Study Bible* (Wheaton, IL: Crossway Bibles, 2008), 31.

[6] Ibid.

[7] Chad Brand, ed., *The Holman Illustrated Bible Dictionary* (Nashville, TN: Thomas Nelson Publishers, 2003), 357.

[8] Ibid.

[9] *ESV Study Bible*, 30.

[10] Ibid., 30.

The New Testament Scriptures make clear that the stipulations of the Mosaic Covenant could not bring about salvation but were *"a shadow of good things to come"* (Hebrews 10:1, KJV). They could only point in symbolic fashion to the sacrifice of Christ on the cross which alone can atone for our sin (Hebrews 10:1–22).

The New Covenant opened the door to *"a new and living way"* (Hebrews 10:20, KJV) when Christ shed His blood on the cross. John MacArthur combines both testaments when he says that "salvation is always by the same gracious means, whether during OT or NT times."[11] The common denominator for both testaments is the cross to which all else is directed. In His own words, the Lord Jesus says that He sealed the deal—the real deal, the Covenant—with His own blood. His work of atonement is remembered every time we observe the ordinance of the Lord's Table (Matthew 26:26–30, 1 Corinthians 11:25–26).

## I WILL BUILD MY CHURCH

Our Lord's earthly odyssey entailed more than thirty-three years. His purpose was to purchase our redemption on the cross and make us part of His bride, the church. This is clearly enunciated in Matthew 16:16–21. Contrasting the New Covenant with the Old, John MacArthur reminds us that "Jesus' death retroactively redeemed all those who had believed in God under the Old Covenant."[12] Speaking of *"they which are called"* (Hebrews 9:15, KJV), he better translates the verse this way:

> the ones having been called which looks back to those under the Old Covenant who were called to salvation by God on the basis of the sacrifice of Jesus Christ to come long after most of them had died.[13]

---

[11] John MacArthur, *The MacArthur Study Bible* (Nashville, TN: Thomas Nelson, 1982), ix.

[12] Ibid., 1911.

[13] Ibid.

The New Covenant, which is the vital essence of the odyssey of grace, was first addressed by Jeremiah (31:27–34) and further echoed by the exilic prophet Ezekiel (36:26–27).

The coming of Christ, in fulfillment of numerous Old Testament prophecies, has had a major impact on the human race. His profound and lasting influence defies an adequate evaluation. In the English language alone, more than one hundred thousand biographies have been written about the carpenter's son from Nazareth (Luke 3:23). The earthly sojourn of Christ ended at His ascension (Acts 1:9), but His faithful followers continued His legacy by engaging in a spiritual missionary enterprise that yet survives and thrives.

## CATCHING THE FIRE

The men Jesus chose to be the leaders of this movement of grace were a motley bunch with none of the credentials we would think necessary for leadership.

The early church was known simply as The Way.[14] For a time, this new sect was granted no official recognition and was virtually ignored by an indifferent society. Some of the disciples were martyred early on. Eventually, all of the twelve, except John, would meet such an end. While some remained close to home, others were well travelled, including Thomas. India today boasts more than twenty-seven million Christians who track their spiritual ancestry to the "doubting disciple." Thomas took the message of Christ to India, and twenty years after his arrival he was martyred there.[15]

The rapid growth of the early church was nothing short of astounding. Columba Stewart, Benedictine monk and historian of Saint John's Abbey in Minnesota, well expresses the unbridled fervency exhibited by these early saints:

---

[14] Paraphrased from Andrew Todhunter's *In the Footsteps of the Apostles* (National Geographic, March 2012, 47).

[15] Ibid., 40–42.

> There was an apostolic band of followers. There were missionary efforts in major centers, first in Jerusalem, then Antioch, then Rome, but certainly no sense of a headquarters. Instead, you had this tiny, vulnerable, poor, often persecuted group of people who were on fire with something.[16]

This Roman Catholic prelate then gives us this vivid assessment of the Apostles:

> The Apostles were the movement's cutting edge, spreading the message across the vast trade network of the ancient world and leaving small Christian communities in their paths. To study the lives of the Apostles is a bit like what we've been doing with the Hubble telescope... getting as close as we can to seeing these earliest galaxies. This was the big bang movement for Christianity, with the Apostles blasting out of Jerusalem and scattering across the known world.[17]

## NEW TESTAMENT DOCUMENTS

The second major division of the Scriptures consists of twenty-seven separate writings called books. The central literature, which set the tone for the remainder of the books, are the four accounts of the life of Christ, called the Gospels. The fourth Gospel is distinct from the other three.

The exciting history of the earliest days of the church can be found in the book of Acts. These five books are followed by twenty-one letters written to individuals or churches. The last book is the Revelation, which is also called the Apocalypse. The last book of the New Testament is described this way: "The apocalypse is a coded message of hope to the church of the first century that has been reinterpreted by each succeeding generation of Christians for their own situations."[18]

[16] Ibid., 48.

[17] Ibid.

[18] Brand, ed., *The Holman Illustrated Bible Dictionary*, 11.

## ANTICIPATION OF THE MESSIAH

The events played out in the thirteen chapters of the Old Testament book of Nehemiah, punctuated by the contemporary ministry of the prophet Malachi, brought finality to the Old Testament canon both historically and prophetically. For more than four hundred years, God's voice fell silent, but His sovereign hand continued to actively direct the course of human events throughout this intertestamental period as He prepared the world for the coming of Messiah.

The thrice-repeated prayer of Nehemiah (Nehemiah 13:14, 22, and 31), which is capsulated in five words, "Remember me, O my God," would be answered both personally (for the Persian king's confidant and cupbearer) and nationally (for the Jewish nation).

God hadn't forgotten His faithful servant, who had been enabled to lead a contingent of His people to repair the gates and walls of Jerusalem in the face of relentless intimidation and ongoing violent opposition from local enemies. By the time we read the closing words in the book of Nehemiah, we are brought to about 410 BC, with God's chosen people having already been brutalized and exiled by the fading empires of Assyria and Babylonia. Now subjugated by the more noble Persians, their scattered remnants would soon be brought into the orbit of the refined and cultured Greeks, whose empire would be precipitated by the military genius of Alexander the Great.

Following Alexander's death in 323 BC, his empire was divided among four of his generals, with the Jews being caught in the middle of a power play between the Ptolemies of Egypt and the Seleucids of Syria.

From 198 BC until 143 BC, Judea was under the Seleucid rule, but the Jews revolted against their overlords following thirty years of relative calm. The oppressive rule of Antiochus Epiphanes IV (175–164 BC), which saw the temple desecrated, Old Testament Scriptures destroyed, idolatrous altars set up, and swine offered up as sacrifices, drove the descendants of Abraham to an all-out revolt in 166 BC.

Independence from Syria was won in 142 BC, but due to continuing Hellenistic (Greek) influence and division among their own people, it became impossible to establish and maintain a stable government. In 63 BC, the foundering nation was annexed to the Roman Empire.[19]

## THE VOICE IN THE WILDERNESS

While the first official Roman emperor, Caesar Augustus, frittered away his final days as the imperial head of the most powerful empire the world had ever witnessed, God was quietly at work among His people in the rolling hills of Judea.

In a beautiful and compelling narrative, Luke 1:5–17 tells of an aged priest called Zacharias and his wife Elisabeth who was at once advanced in years and barren. They had no child, but in response to the promise of God they would soon become parents to a baby boy called John. Known to us as John the Baptist, his ministry would become the watershed of the Old Testament laws and prophets and prepare his people for the promised Redeemer and the New Covenant (Matthew 11:13 and Luke 16:26).

In precise detail, Luke records how Elisabeth sought privacy during the first five months of her pregnancy; during her sixth month, the angel Gabriel announced to the unmarried and pregnant Virgin Mary that she would soon give birth to the Son of God. Mary and Elisabeth were relatives and throughout Luke 1 their lives and experiences are closely intertwined. Both parents of John the Baptist were from the priestly line of Aaron, but their son was destined to abandon the priesthood and take up a life of asceticism in the Judean wilderness, where he subsisted on a diet of locusts and wild honey (Mark 1:6).

Dressed in the attire of an Old Testament prophet (2 Kings 1:8), John preached a powerful message of repentance and baptized his converts in the River Jordan following their confession of sin. On one of these occasions, he was approached by the Lord Jesus, who requested baptism. Following a vehement protest, John submitted to his Lord's desire, baptizing the Lord Jesus in front of the throngs of people along the riverbank. Then God the Father spoke from heaven and the Holy Spirit descended upon our Lord Jesus as a dove.

[19] Ibid., 850.

All of this is recorded for us in Matthew 3. Since John and Jesus were related and were apparently very familiar with each other, I've often wondered if they played together as boys. I have also been curious to know whether John's parents lived long enough to hear him preach. This is highly unlikely due to their advanced age at the time of his birth.

What we do know is that John's ministry centered on the Messiah to come. He was always careful to remind his hearers that he was only a voice in the wilderness, constantly pointing them to the Lord Jesus whom he referred to as *"the Lamb of God who takes away the sin of the world"* (John 1:29, NKJV).

Huge crowds came as he reminded them that religious ceremony, lineal descent from Abraham, and ancestral heritage did nothing to curry the favour of God. His offer of salvation to rich and poor, including prostitutes and tax collectors, did a great deal to stir the wrath of the religious traditionalists of the day; they were stung by his boldness of delivery and courage of conviction as he denounced sin of every form and issued a stern warning about the coming wrath of God. Following a blistering rebuke of Herod Antipas for cohabiting with his brother's wife, John was imprisoned and eventually beheaded.

With many ministries today placing strong emphasis on the miraculous, including physical healing, it is of interest to note that John didn't perform a single miracle according to John 10:41. To further support the argument that God places no premium on the ability to perform miracles, the Lord Jesus reminds us that *"among those born of women there is not a greater prophet than John the Baptist"* (Luke 7:28, NKJV).

John's greatness isn't measured in signs and wonders, of which there are none, but rather by a lasting legacy of truthfulness and faithfulness (John 10:41) that prepared the Jewish nation for the coming of the Messiah and helped lay the groundwork for the church He came to build (Matthew 16:18).

## A RICH SOURCE OF REDEMPTIVE TRUTH

Unlike much of modern theology, which to my mind is sorely lacking in Old Testament content, the biblical message of God's plan of redemption betrays a close affinity between the Old and New Testaments. They fit together like hand in glove. From Genesis 3:15, with the promise that the seed of the woman would triumph over the seed of the serpent until the final amen of Revelation 22:21, God's message and plan remain ever the same. It cannot be overemphasized that the historical events of Genesis are pivotal to our understanding of God's program as it unfolds throughout the other sixty-five books of the Bible. To throw doubt upon the truth of Genesis is to undermine the entire body of Scripture, and to put the very words of Christ in disrepute, as He quoted from this book of beginnings on numerous occasions.

The promise of God's saving grace is carefully developed in the Old Testament covenants. There is His covenant with Noah, in which He promised to never again flood the earth (Genesis 9:9–17). Secondly, there is His covenant with Abraham by which He promised His people land, seed, and universal blessing (Genesis 12:1–3). Thirdly, there is His covenant with Moses whereby He pledges His blessing to Israel in response to their obedience (Exodus 19–24). Fourthly, there is God's covenant with David by which a king is promised through his family line forever; the promises originally made to Abraham became a reality as they threaded their way through the Davidic line (2 Samuel 7, Psalm 89, 132).

Lastly, embedded in the New Covenant, is the promise that God will give His Spirit to His people and write His law on their hearts so they would of their own volition obey His will (Jeremiah 31:31–34, Ezekiel 36:26–27). This better covenant is more fully explored in the New Testament book of Hebrews, where Christ is presented as our great High Priest (Hebrews 3:1).

We are given a continuous reminder of this New Covenant in Matthew 26:26–29 as the Lord Jesus institutes the Lord's Supper.[20]

[20] Ibid., 356–357.

# Introduction

We now move on to a review of the canon known as the New Testament where the last Adam (1 Corinthians 15:45), as the offspring of Abraham, comes to us clothed in human flesh, lives among us as perfect man and perfect God, dies for us at a place called Calvary, and rises from the dead on the third day, thus reversing the effects of Adam's fall, fulfilling numerous Old Testament prophecies and securing salvation full and free for all who will embrace Him and trust Him by faith. It is impossible to find enough words to fully describe the impact Christ has made on the human race.

The following article is one person's attempt to help us grasp, in some small measure, the lasting effect Christ has had on the human race. The author was James Allen Francis, born in Upper Stewiacke, Nova Scotia on March 20, 1864. Having received a common school education, he entered the ministry and became the pastor of Riverside Baptist Church in New York City in 1891. He later accepted the pastorate of Clarendon St. Church in Boston, and then moved to Los Angeles in 1914 to commence a fourteen-year ministry.

On a Sunday evening in 1927, Francis delivered the sermon of dedication for a new sanctuary for the First Baptist Church of Los Angeles. It was on this occasion that "One Solitary Life" was heard for the very first time. So well was it received that it was published almost immediately. This riveting piece of literature often appears anonymously as a streamlined version. The rendition here is the longer original as given by this famed author and former Nova Scotian who passed away on June 30, 1928.

## ONE SOLITARY LIFE

**H**ere is a man who was born in an obscure village, the Child of a peasant woman. He worked in a carpenter's shop until he was thirty, and then for three years he was an itinerate preacher.

**H**e never wrote a book. He never held an office. He never owned a home. He never had a family. He never went to college. He never put his foot inside a big city. He never travelled two hundred miles from the place where he was born.

**H**e never did one of the things that usually accompany greatness. He had no credentials but Himself. He had nothing to do with this world except the naked power of His Divine manhood.

**W**hile still a young man, the tide of popular opinion turned against Him. He was turned over to His enemies. He went through the mockery of a trial. He was nailed to a cross between two thieves. His executioners gambled for the only piece of property He had on earth while He was dying—and that was His coat.

**W**hen He was dead He was taken down and laid in a borrowed grave through the pity of a friend. Then He arose—man's triumph over death and sin!

> **N**ineteen wide centuries have come and gone and today He is the Centerpiece of the human race and the Leader of the column of progress.
>
> **I** am within the mark when I say that all the armies that every marched, and all the navies that ever were built, and all the parliaments that ever sat, and all the kings that ever reigned, put together, have not affected the life of man upon this world as powerfully as that One Solitary Life.[21]
>
> —James Allen Francis, D.D., LL.D.

The four Gospels are the usual designation for the inspired biographies that introduce the New Testament. From the Scripture record, we learn that the term Gospel references the good news of salvation for a lost humanity made available through the life, death, and resurrection of Jesus Christ, the God-man. The word Gospel is a contraction of an old English word, Godspell, which means "news about God." This is the Old English rendering of the Greek word *euaggelion*, or *Evangelium*, from which we derive the word evangel and evangelism.

It is well for us to note here that the Gospel, as fleshed out in the Scriptures, is far more than a mental assent to historical facts. The essence of the Gospel is laid out for us in 1 Corinthians 15, where the Apostle Paul features the death, burial, and resurrection of Christ as the centrepiece of his message. For the sinner to receive salvation, they must do more than accept these facts intellectually; there must have faith and trust in the Christ who died and rose again from the dead, inviting Him to come into their hearts and transform them by His grace. This is clearly borne out in Romans 10:9–11, where the writer accents the vital importance of mouth confession and heart belief.

---

[21] James Allen Francis, "One Solitary Life," *The Baptist Beacon*, December 1992, 11–12.

## I NEVER KNEW YOU

We are in a day of easy-believism that allows Christians to live as they please and give little proof of being any different from the unsaved around them. The contemporary Christian has been lulled into believing that because they signed a card, recited a prayer, walked to the front of the church, spoke in tongues, or went through some other experience or formality, we must never question their profession of faith even if it demonstrates no repentance, transformation, fruit of the spirit, or any other evidence that signal a true conversion.

A careful reading of Matthew 7:21–23 tells of a group of professing Christians who have what we would consider all the earmarks of genuine conversion. The words of their lips sound so convincing as they mouth repeatedly the words of Lordship. Their activities seem to evidence a life of genuine religious energy, resulting in what appears to be marvelous and miraculous phenomena. In the name of the Lord they profess to know, their lips utter words of prophecy. With the repeated injunction "in your name," they are enabled to challenge demons and cast them out, exercising the name of the God they claim to represent. Extraordinary powers are manifested through them. Everything looks so real and genuine.

But there is one fatal flaw, it hits us like a sledgehammer—not one of these professing Christians has been to Calvary and experienced salvation through faith in Jesus Christ. They have never known a born again experience. They are false prophets who exist in the church with their own fleshly agenda. Rather than serving the Lord Jesus, they only use His blessed name to boost their own ego and magnify their self-importance.

These are not Christians who have had an experience with God, then lost their way, only to finally perish in the end. The wording in the Bible is very clear: these counterfeit converts approach Jesus Himself, and they are weighed in the balance and found wanting. The terrible and fearful words "I never knew you" must surely have come to these self-made prophets with shocking reality. It's a powerful refutation of all they profess to be. The truth is that they have never in their lifetime had an experience with God. They are not born again and have never been washed in the blood.

The final blow is dealt with a deafening roar straight from the throne of God: *"[D]epart from me, ye that work iniquity"* (Matthew 7:23, KJV). Like the magicians of Egypt, who were able to duplicate the miracles of Moses, these self-righteous hypocrites remained inwardly unchanged. They remained in bondage to their own sinful desires while neatly covering their tracks with an endless round of religious activity (Exodus 7:11, 22; 8:7).

The words of MacArthur get straight to the point:

> The Gospel Jesus proclaimed was a call to discipleship, a call to follow Him in submissive obedience, not just a plea to make a decision or pray a prayer. Jesus' message liberated people from the bondage of their sin while it confronted and condemned hypocrisy. It was an offer of eternal life and forgiveness for repentant sinners, but at the same time, it was a rebuke to outwardly religious people whose lives were devoid of true righteousness. It put sinners on notice that they must turn from sin and embrace God's righteousness. It was in every sense, good news, yet it was anything but easy-believism. Our Lord's words about eternal life were invariably accompanied by warnings to those who might be tempted to take salvation lightly. He taught that the cost of following Him was high, that the way is narrow and few find it. He said many who will call Him Lord will be forbidden from entering the kingdom of heaven." (Cf. Matthew 7:13–23)[22]

We will now move on to a closer examination of the four Gospels, followed by the other twenty-three books of the New Testament. Each

[22] John MacArthur Jr., *The Gospel According to Jesus* (Grand Rapids, MI: Zondervan, 1988), 21.

of the Gospel writers has a perspective that is uniquely different from the other three, and each addresses a different audience. Each Gospel contains distinctive elements, and taken together they form a balanced and complete testimony about Jesus Christ.

# The Gospel According to Matthew

The author of the book is Matthew, who is also called Levi. It is quite probable that Levi was Matthew's name before he became a disciple of Christ. The name Matthew means "gift of the Lord."

There are twenty-eight chapters in the Gospel of Matthew broken into:

- The Genealogy of Jesus Christ (1:1–17).
- The Conception and Birth of Christ (1:18–25).
- The Wise Men and the Slaughter of the Innocents (2:1–23).
- John the Baptist and the Baptism of Christ (3:1–17).
- The Temptation of Christ and the Beginning of His Ministry (4:1–25).
- The Sermon on the Mount (5:1–7:29).
- The Centurion's Faith and Christ's Visit to Gadara (8:1–34)
- The Calling of Matthew and Miracles of Healing (9:1–38)
- The Twelve Disciples and the Meaning of Discipleship (10:1–42)
- A Tribute to John the Baptist (11:1–30)

- The Sabbath, the Unpardonable Sin, and Signs (12:1–50)
- Eight Parables (13:1–58)
- John the Baptist Beheaded (14:1–12)
- The Five Thousand Fed, Jesus Walks on the Water (14:13–36)
- Tradition and the Syrophoenician Woman (15:1–39)
- Building the Church (16:1–28)
- The Transfiguration and Forgiveness (17:1–18:35)
- Divorce and Labourers in the Vineyard (19:1–20:34)
- The Triumphal Entry (21:1–46).
- Sadducees and the Seven Woes (22:1–23:39).
- The Return of Christ and Signs (24:1–51).
- The Ten Virgins and the Talents (25:1–46).
- The Plot to Kill Jesus (26:1–75).
- The Crucifixion and Related Events (27:1–66).
- The Resurrection and the Great Commission (28:1–20).

We have already made reference to the word *Godspell* from which we derive Gospel. In concert with the Greek from which we extract the word evangelism, we deduct the meaning of "news or a story about God" or "a good story." The root word for evangelism refers to a good report about an important event. In the words of one writer, "the four Gospels are the good news about the most significant event in all of history—the life, sacrificial death, and resurrection of Jesus of Nazareth."[23]

The summary will attempt to capture the flow of the book as it moves along, point our interest to the more significant portions of Scripture, and deal in some measure with those passages that have engendered controversy. Since some of the most intellectual and spiritual minds have been unable to come to full agreement in some areas of biblical teaching, I'm not going to be so brazen as to offer a final solution for difficult passages; they will continue to challenge our very limited, finite minds.

There are times when a forceful and unyielding dogmatism must give way to a gentleness of spirit, allowing for the acceptance of a variety

[23] MacArthur, *The MacArthur Study Bible*, 1375.

of views as believers grapple with the greatest volume of writings ever entrusted to the human race. Mark Twain once remarked that he had long ago ceased to worry about the things he did not know but was greatly exercised about the things he did know.[24]

Some aspects of Scripture just aren't as clear as one would like them to be, and I've long ago concluded that some issues will not be fully settled this side of heaven. These words from Deuteronomy 29:29 can be a source of great encouragement as we grapple with some of the deep truths and intricate details of God's Word: *"The secret things belong unto the Lord our God: but those things which are revealed belong unto us and to our children for ever, that we may do all the words of this law"* (KJV).

## SUMMARY

Because they share a common point of view about Christ and focus on our Lord's ministry in Galilee, Matthew, Mark, and Luke's writings are commonly referred to as the synoptic Gospels. The word synopsis comes from the Greek and means "to see together" or "to share a common point of view." The Gospel of John is in a different category from the other three with its focus on the ministry of Christ in Judea rather than Galilee. There are numerous parables throughout the first three Gospels while there are none in the Gospel of John.

Matthew wrote primarily to a Jewish audience, presenting Jesus of Nazareth as the promised Messiah and rightful king of Israel. As a former tax collector, Matthew took a keen interest in names, occupations, family status, and ancestral lineage, which probably best explains why the first seventeen verses of his Gospel are given over to the genealogy of the Lord Jesus Christ.

Another genealogical table is found in Luke 3, with some readers questioning why there are obvious differences between the two. They are easily reconciled when we realize that Matthew's line of descent

---

[24] J. Stephen Lang, *1,001 Things You Always Wanted to Know About the Bible But Never Thought to Ask* (Nashville, TN: Nelson Books, 1999), 367.

comes through Joseph while Luke's comes through Mary, working backward from Jesus to Adam. With his record moving forward from Abraham to Joseph, Matthew includes women in his account while women are excluded from that of Luke. Even though Luke's line of descent is through Mary, her name is omitted from the record.

The Gospels do not intend to present a complete account of the life of Christ, but together they do provide a complete testimony about Christ in written form. The quartet of Gospel writers are not biographers in the modern sense, and with the exception of the birth narratives there is very little material given to us about the first thirty years of the life of Christ. His public ministry encompassed about three and a half years and the Gospel accounts are primarily occupied with the last week of His life.

However, we are all familiar with the account in Matthew 1:18–2:23, which, coupled with the beautifully written narrative in Luke 2, is the only window we are given into the events that surround the birth of Christ. In this passage, five dreams are recorded (Matthew 1:20; 2:12, 13, 19, 22).

Only in Matthew's Gospel do we find the account of the wise men and Mary and Joseph's flight into Egypt when Herod vented his wrath by murdering all the male babies under two years of age in Bethlehem and the surrounding area.

Matthew 2:11–16 shatters all our Christmas images of the manger scene, images which show the shepherds and wise men hovering together over the baby Jesus. By the time these Persian astrologers arrived in Bethlehem, the young child was nearly two years old and living with His parents in their own home.

The ministry of John the Baptist has already been covered. Following His baptism in Matthew 3:16, Jesus was led by the Spirit into the wilderness to be tempted by the devil, where Satan's temptations were met with a number of Scriptures quoted by our Lord. The words *"[f]rom that time Jesus began to preach"* (Matthew 4:17, KJV) signal the commencement of our Lord's public ministry.

Matthew is the only writer to employ the phrase "kingdom of heaven," which is used repeatedly beginning with Matthew 3:2 and is interchangeable with the phrase "kingdom of God" in the other Gospels. Some scholars differ here.

The subject of Matthew 5:1–7:29 is the famous Sermon on the Mount. Over the past one hundred fifty years, this passage has suffered at the hands of Bible scholars who feel it is so centered on the Law that its emphasis belongs in the millennial reign. This is where some extreme elements of dispensational teaching, which I'll deal with more fully when we cover the book of Revelation, have in my opinion gone off the rail. The subject matter dealt with here belongs to the present age, not to some future kingdom age with no relevance to the present.

One writer has offered the following summation:

> This sermon is a masterful exposition of the Law and a potent assault on Pharisaic legalism, closing with a call to true faith and salvation. Christ expounded the full meaning of the Law showing that its demands were humanly impossible. This is the proper use of the Law with respect to salvation: it closes off every possible avenue of human merit and leaves sinners dependant on nothing but divine grace for salvation. Christ plumbed the depth of the Law, showing that its true demands went far beyond the surface meaning of the words and set a standard that is higher than the most diligent students of the Law had heretofore realized.[25]

We aren't certain of the exact location of the mount where this sermon was preached, but the traditional site has been a high ridge northwest of the town of Capernaum.

This powerful message is introduced with the nine blessings, which have become known as the Beatitudes (Matthew 5:1–11). The word beatitude is derived from the Latin word *beatus*, which is the

---

[25] MacArthur, *The MacArthur Study Bible*, 1399.

equivalent of *blessed* and means "divinely bestowed well being" or "blessed." These short and pithy statements are a summary of the basic essence of the Sermon on the Mount. The sermon covers a variety of subjects including murder, divorce, adultery, oaths, prayer, wealth, and judging.

Matthew 8 consists of a number of miracles performed by the Lord Jesus following His descent from the mount. A leper is cleansed, a centurion's servant is healed, Peter's mother-in-law is healed, the sea is stilled, and demons are cast into swine. Matthew 9:9 tells of the call of Matthew to discipleship as he was sitting in his tax office. The twelve disciples are called, instructed, and sent out shortly thereafter. We then see the ministry of John the Baptist endorsed by the Lord Jesus.

In Matthew 12 we encounter a strong movement to kill the Lord Jesus, with the Pharisees leading the way. The content of Matthew 12:40 is stated only in this Gospel and has created no end of discussion. How does this verse square with a Friday crucifixion followed by an early Sunday morning resurrection?

## THE THREE DAYS AND THREE NIGHTS OF JONAH

> *For as Jonas was three days and three nights in the whale's belly; so shall the Son of man be three days and three nights in the heart of the earth.* (Matthew 12:40, NKJV)

This verse has caused a great deal of discussion among Bible students, with some suggesting there seems to be a contradiction. Since Jesus was crucified on a Friday afternoon and rose from the dead on Sunday morning, how can this verse be true? There just isn't enough time.

Over the years, some have done theological handstands in order to satisfy the demands of this verse. Some have gone to great lengths to prove a Wednesday crucifixion or a Thursday crucifixion.

At one time, Ralph Woodrow was convinced that Jesus was crucified on a Wednesday and arose on Saturday. After many years, he became convinced that this was not in concordance with the Bible; he has since returned to the standard belief that Jesus was crucified on a Friday and arose from the grave on Sunday morning.[26]

Another explanation is that the ancient Jews often referred to a part of a day or night to refer to a complete day-night cycle, but this has never been satisfactory to me. Rather, this verse refers back to Jonah in the Old Testament. Jesus seems to have been very precise time, and in literal terms this period encompassed seventy-two hours.[27]

Matthew 12:40 is the only verse that makes this statement. The three day, three night scenario is noticeably absent from the other Gospels.

The Scriptures are very precise about the resurrection, which took place on the third day, which by all accounts was Sunday morning. The following verses are clear and unified: Matthew 16:21; 17:23; 20:19; 26:61; 27:40, 64; Mark 9:31; 10:34; 14:58; 15:29; Luke 9:22; 13:32; 18:33; 24:7, 21, 46; John 2:19–20; Acts 10:40; and 1 Corinthians 15:4.

By taking this verse at face value, we must note what is seen here and what isn't seen. Notice that there is not one word about the crucifixion or death of Christ. There is nothing here about the resurrection. These events may be implied, but they are not mentioned per se. Notice, too, that the heart of the earth is not defined or described. This expression is used only by Matthew

---

[26] Ralph Woodrow, *Three Days, Three Nights* (Palm Springs, CA: Ralph Woodrow Evangelistic Association, 2004), 2–4.

[27] Dr. Henry Morris, *The Henry Morris Study Bible* (Green Forest, AR: Master Books, 2012), 1411.

and is found nowhere else in the Scriptures, which means we have no precedent to work from. It stands alone.[28]

Take a moment to read Ezekiel 5:5 and 38:12. In these verses, Jerusalem is referred to as the centre of the world. In the time of Christ, we know the Jews often referred to their royal city as the centre of the world, the heart or navel of the earth.

When did the suffering begin for the Lord Jesus? We know He suffered on the cross, but His suffering in the garden of Gethsemane was so intense that the Scriptures tell us He sweat great drops of blood. This was on Thursday, the day before His death on the cross.

It has been falsely assumed by some that Jesus entered into the abyss of hell between His death on the cross and His resurrection on Sunday morning, but such is not found in the Scriptures. His suffering was completed on the cross when He became a substitute for us. Later, in Matthew 26:46, the Lord Jesus speaks of being betrayed into the hands of sinners, which was the beginning of His horrible ordeal.

The sign Jesus spoke of in reference to Jonah wasn't so much about His suffering, or even His resurrection, but rather the length of time. The last week of His earthly ministry prior to the resurrection was spent in or around the heart of Jerusalem, the centre of the earth. His suffering began there and ended there less than a week after His triumphal entry on Palm Sunday.[29]

His suffering began on Thursday as He wept in Gethsemane, followed by His betrayal by Judas. This was His first day of suffering, and it continued through the night when He was brought to trial. On Friday He was crucified, and on Friday night, Saturday, and Saturday night His body lay in the grave

---

[28] Ibid., 44.

[29] Ibid., 46–48.

until His glorious resurrection early on Sunday morning, the third day. This timeframe covers three days and three nights, which exactly matches what is said in Matthew 12:40.

Woodrow reminds us,

> Every Friday was preparation day (John 19:42), but the Friday on which Jesus died was also the preparation of the Passover (verse 14). As the Jewish people were killing lambs in preparation for the Passover feast, Christ our Passover was sacrificed for us (Cor. 1:5–7). And so He died according to the scriptures on the 14th day of the month, as our Passover.[30]

The writings of the church fathers aren't inspired, but they were close in time to the apostles. All of them taught that the resurrection took place on Sunday, not on the Sabbath.[31]

According to *The New Bible Dictionary*, a parable (from the Greek *parabole*) is "a short descriptive story, usually designed to inculcate a single truth or answer a single truth."[32] This type of storytelling was very common among the Jews of Jesus' day, but the Lord Jesus employed His own unique purpose in the telling of parables. They were used to make truth clearer to His disciples and to hide that same truth from unbelievers.

Forty parables are found in the synoptic Gospels, with eight of them found in Matthew 13, and they are known as the kingdom parables. In Matthew 14, we find the feeding of the five thousand, the only miracle recorded in all four Gospels. Matthew 15 deals with the debate over

[30] Ibid., 32.

[31] Ibid., 28–29.

[32] *The New Bible Dictionary* (Downers Grove: IL, IVP Academic, 1996), 867.

tradition as well as the healing of a Gentile woman's daughter in the region of Tyre and Sidon.

In Matthew 16:13–20, the Lord Jesus employs two probing questions in order to help His disciples become fully aware of His true identity. The rather unstable and impulsive Peter offers a rapid-fire response to the second question: *"You are the Christ, the Son of the living God"* (Matthew 16:16, NKJV). Using this reply as a foundational statement, the Lord Jesus reveals to His followers that He has come to build His church, an impregnable force that would withstand even the onslaughts of Hell. Matthew's Gospel is the only one where the term *church* is found, and it means "called out ones."

A careful reading of this passage, as well as Peter's own writings (1 Peter 2:5–7), will attest to the fact that Peter himself is not the head of the church. Peter himself recognized his own weak and sinful condition and denied his Lord three times as Christ was being tried and convicted of treason. For the Roman Catholic Church to make claim to being the only true church and maintain that the Pope of Rome has an authoritative position that can be traced back to Peter is, in every way, fully contradictory to the truth of God's Word. As the head of His church, the Lord Jesus shares His position with nobody, including the Papacy in Rome.

We wonder why the Popes and priesthood of the Roman Catholic Church are forbidden to marry when even the first Pope, as claimed by them, was a married man who witnessed the healing of his mother-in-law (Matthew 8:14). God has endowed all of us with a natural sexual instinct that is to find its ultimate fulfillment in the marriage bed as one man and one woman commit to a lifetime of faithfulness, often resulting in God's gift of procreation. To deny anyone, whether in ministry or not, the opportunity to enter into the marriage covenant, which God has both established and sanctioned, is both unnatural and unscriptural (1 Timothy 4:1–5, Hebrews 13:4).

Much of Matthew 17 is taken up with the transfiguration of Christ, as well as instructions on faith, death, and taxes. Nearly one half of

Matthew 18 is devoted to the matter of forgiveness, which is ignored by many Christians and often neglected by our churches. Forgiveness allows us to dispel anger, resentment, and the spirit of vindictiveness that often runs rampant in Christian circles.

In Matthew 19, the hot button issue of divorce and remarriage is dealt with, and the blessing of the children and Jesus' conversation with the rich young ruler rounds out the chapter. Matthew 20 deals firstly with the parable of the labourers, followed shortly by the proud and self-seeking ambitions of the two sons of Zebedee. Possibly building their case from the words of Christ in Matthew 19:28, and using their mother as their spokesperson, they made their pitch for an exalted position in the kingdom in order to exercise dominance over the other disciples (Mark 10:35–45). With unabashed boldness, this threesome determined to secure a strong family influence in God's kingdom.

Matthew 21:1 brings us to the triumphal entry, which inaugurates the final week of our Saviour's earthly ministry prior to the resurrection. The cleansing of the temple recorded in this chapter is the second such incident, with John 2:14–16 recording the first such purging at the beginning of Christ's ministry.

The parable of the two sons and the parable of the landowner are also found in this passage.

Matthew 22:1–23:39 records the increasing conflict between the Lord Jesus and the religious factions of the day, including the Sadducees, Herodians, Pharisees, and the Scribes. The last three verses of Matthew 23 then tell of the lament of the Lord Jesus over the city of Jerusalem, which had rejected the Messiah and would shortly cooperate in His condemnation, allowing the Roman authorities to execute Him on a cross outside the city walls. The words of judgment are pronounced in Matthew 23:38: *"See, your house is left to you desolate"* (ESV).

A careful reading of the latter part of Matthew's Gospel tells of Jesus entering the temple in 21:12 and remaining there until His departure in 24:1. In this same verse, the disciples approach the Lord Jesus and point His attention to the beauty and grandeur of the buildings on the Temple Mount. In Matthew 24:2, they must have been shocked and amazed to learn from Jesus that the temple and all its surrounding structures would shortly be utterly destroyed. With stunning exactness and detailed accuracy, He informed them that the day would come when *"[t]here shall not be left here one stone upon another, that shall not be thrown down"* (Matthew 24:2, NKJV).

It was common in New Testament times for teachers to take a seated position while instructing their students, which explains why the Lord Jesus takes time to rest on the Mount of Olives and instruct His disciples. From Matthew 24:3 to 25:46, He gives what is commonly known as the Olivet Discourse.

This passage is a powerful statement about future events, but it's not without controversy among students of Scripture. I will only touch lightly on some aspects of this Scripture and will spend little time on some of its more debateable interpretations and ramifications.

Many may be surprised to learn that there are varied opinions on such things as the kingdom, the great tribulation, the thousand-year reign, and even the second coming of Christ. Is there one coming or two? My own position on future events is far from settled. I don't believe that prophetical differences should be a basis for the disruption of fellowship between Christians. When we summarize the book of Revelation, I will share some of the more significant views and major schools of interpretation.

Whatever view we hold regarding future events, some aspects of this discourse are abundantly clear. The world is destined to experience one catastrophic event after another throughout its history. There will be scores of false Christs and numerous dysfunctional religious systems that have little or no resemblance to the Christian faith. False prophets will follow one another in rapid succession. They will come with great signs and wonders and, if possible, deceive the very elect of God. Our Lord Jesus is coming again in great power and glory and we are asked to be always ready for His appearing.

Whether the calamitous events in Matthew 24 are close at hand to the time Christ spoke, were seen throughout the history of the church, or are a part of a seven-year tribulation era that is still to come, there is full agreement that the destruction of the city of Jerusalem and the temple took place in AD 70, with the words of Christ being fulfilled in graphic detail. Ralph Woodrow describes the scene:

> Figuring from the time Vespasian received his commission from Nero and declared war on Jerusalem (February, AD 67) until the end of the siege and destruction of the city and temple (August, AD 70), this treading down of Jerusalem—in actual time—was three and a half years.[33]

The same writer takes us back to the previous destruction of the city:

> Highly significant is the fact that the very date on which the temple was burned by the armies of Titus was the same date that Nebuchadnezzar had burned it centuries before! But, as for that house, God had for certain long ago doomed it to the fire, and now that fatal day was come, according to the revolution of the ages; it was the tenth day of the month Abib, upon which it was formerly burnt by the king of Babylon.[34]

As the temple was pillaged and torched by the Roman armies, the heat became so intense that some of the temple gold became liquefied and ran down between the stones where it hardened. So intent were the Romans on extracting this gold from the foundation stones that they pried the stones apart in order to salvage the treasure, an exact fulfillment of Matthew 24:2.

---

[33] Ralph Woodrow, *Great Prophecies of the Bible* (Palm Springs, CA: Ralph Woodrow Evangelistic Association, 1999), 68.

[34] Ibid., 63.

Some historians have recorded that not a single Christian perished in this military assault on the city of David.[35] They had heard and believed the words of Christ nearly forty years earlier, and when they realized the futility of further resistance to the Roman armies they took their families, escaped the city, and fled to Pella and other retreats beyond the River Jordan.[36]

Much has been made about the meaning of the parable of the ten virgins in Matthew 25:1–13. Perhaps too much has been read into this beautiful picture of a Jewish marriage ceremony, which would have been very familiar to those listening in the time of Christ. Possibly the most basic lesson to be learned here is that we must watch correctly and in a discerning manner in order to be "properly prepared and ready to accompany the Son of Man when He returns."[37]

Reading the parable of the talents in Matthew 25:14–30 can be puzzling to the modern reader. There were no banks in ancient times, and valuables were buried in the ground for safekeeping. This parable points to the importance of faithful service to God by using all that is entrusted to us for His glory. We are to await His coming with diligence and patience. We also learn that we are not judged according to the amount we earn but on how we use and invest that which has been granted to us.

The final segment of this chapter, Matthew 25:31–46, concerns judgment and the final destiny of all who stand before the throne of God. Some believe this is a separate judgment from the Great White Throne Judgment or the Judgment Seat of Christ. Along with this view is the belief that the "brothers" mentioned in Matthew 25:40 are representative of the nation of Israel and that these nations are to be judged in relation to their treatment of the Jews. Whether this is a separate judgment or not, I remain unconvinced that the brothers in Matthew 25:40 are Jews. I have concluded that these "brothers" refer

---

[35] Ibid., 54.

[36] Ibid., 53–54.

[37] *ESV Study Bible*, 1876. See notation Matthew 25:13.

to the most needy among believers. They are most likely disciples of Christ, no matter their nationality.

The verse also provides a lesson about our motives. We do not perform compassionate deeds to be accepted by our Lord, but our good works are to flow out of a life that has been transformed by the grace of God. This parable perfectly illustrates the concepts presented in Ephesians 2:8–10.

From Matthew 26:1–28:20, events move at breakneck speed, beginning with the plot to put Jesus to death and ending with His glorious resurrection. While Jesus was visiting at the home of Simon the Leper, He was anointed with a flask of expensive and fragrant oil. Moving further into Matthew 26, we see Judas cutting a deal with the chief priests to betray his Master for thirty pieces of silver.

The actions of Judas and the chief priests fulfill the words of Zechariah 11:12–13. The Lord Jesus was then joined by all His disciples, including Judas, in Matthew 26:17. Jesus had made prior arrangements to eat the Passover at a specified home in Jerusalem, and His followers were sent ahead of Him for the preparation with a gripping and cryptic message for their host: *"My time is at hand"* (Matthew 26:18, KJV). This statement brings into clear focus what His mission was all about. As He made His way from Bethany to Jerusalem, He determined to both embrace and fulfill the great plan of the ages (Revelation 13:8).

## A MOST UNUSUAL NIGHT

The night preceding the crucifixion of Christ was like no other, before or since. As our Lord reclined with His twelve chosen men in Matthew 26:20, the religious constabulary was determining His execution, and they moved as swiftly and expeditiously as possible. All of their previous attempts had been frustrated, but not this time.

The night would soon devolve into incessant deception, bribery, interrogation, and devious political string-pulling in order to bring about the murder of the Messiah.

As Jesus entered into the Passover with the twelve at about 6:00 p.m. on Thursday evening, He dropped a bombshell, warning them of the impending storm. At least three times in the past (Matthew 16:21), He had advised His disciples how things would wind up, but on this occasion He added a troubling detail. One as yet unnamed member of the inner circle would betray Him into the hands of the authorities, thus providing the catalyst that would lead to His execution. A hush settled over the assembled men as they tried to identify the guilty party.

Some scholars refer to this occasion as the last Passover, but it should more properly be referred to as the last valid Passover. The Apostle Paul reminds us in 1 Corinthians 5:7 that Christ has fulfilled the Old Testament sacrifices and is now our Passover. The Jews who disowned the claims of Christ continued their blood sacrifices until the destruction of the temple in 70 AD, which had been prophesied by Christ in Matthew 24:1–2.

Four cups were observed at the Passover feast, and as they partook of what was most likely the third cup (Matthew 26:27), Jesus transformed this particular Passover into the first observance of the Lord's Supper.[38] As we read Matthew 26:28–29, we note that this cup becomes a dynamic symbol of the shed blood of Christ.

The followers of Christ have commemorated the Lord's Supper ever since, as an ongoing testimony to the validity of the Christian faith. A careful reading of the New Testament Scriptures reveal that the term "wine" is never used in reference to the Lord's supper; the cup contained the fruit of the vine, fresh grape juice.[39]

A comparison of the Gospel accounts indicates that Judas slipped away prior to the institution of the Lord's Supper, during the Passover portion of the evening, with the other men taking little notice of his absence.[40] This would put the timing between of Judas' exit around Matthew 26:25–26.

---

[38] John MacArthur, *The Murder of Jesus* (Nashville, TN: Word Publishing, 2000), 39–40.

[39] *ESV Study Bible*, 1881. See notations Matthew 26:26–26:28.

[40] MacArthur, *The Murder of Jesus*, 35–37.

John 13:26–30 records some of the riveting details of this darkest of moments in human history. The task of betrayal wasn't left for Judas alone. In John 13:27, Satan personally took command of the situation by indwelling the bodily frame of Judas. John seems to stress the time of day in John 13:30—*"and it was night"* (KJV).

The wheels were now turning to have Jesus arrested and tried.

The suggestion by some that Jesus was misunderstood by the Jewish authorities is clearly off the mark. They fully grasped everything He said, which explains their determination to have Him eliminated. By word and deed, He unabashedly declared that He was God and Messiah. While Christ was embraced by many, He was largely rejected by the religious leaders of the time. His miracles, including the rising of Lazarus after four days in the grave, could not be easily refuted (John 11). The religious leaders' refusal to acknowledge His claims soon turned to anger and hatred. They were jealous of His large following and became bent on His destruction.

In the time of Jesus, the Supreme Court of Israel was the Sanhedrin, consisting of seventy-one members. From a technical standpoint, they were prohibited by Roman law from administering the death penalty. Persons deemed deserving of death for a capital offense were to be turned over to the Roman authorities for trial and punishment.[41] Capital punishment was a common expedient in Roman courts of law, but sometimes the Romans ignored the actions of their subjects and turned a blind eye to restrictions on the death penalty. When Stephan was stoned by the Jews in Acts 6:8–15, the Romans turned the other way.

Following their time of singing in John 13:30, Jesus and His disciples made their way to the Mount of Olives. From this vantage point, which rose two hundred feet above the temple precinct, Jesus quoted from Zechariah 13:7, telling His followers that every last one of them would forsake Him that very night. He further reminded them of His resurrection, which brought the disciples' minds to ponder the unthinkable: His impending death. Peter protested firmly, but he was

---

[41] MacArthur, *MacArthur Study Bible*, 1446. See notation Matthew 26:59.

told that he would deny Christ no less than three times before the rooster crowed in the morning.

They then settled for a time in Gethsemane. While the disciples succumbed to sleep, the Lord Jesus agonized in prayer on three separate occasions. The evening was wearing on and by the time they made their exit from the garden it was most probably around midnight.

## THE KISS OF BETRAYAL

They were met almost immediately by what can only be described as a mixed mob that had been joined, or at least followed, by curious onlookers, including the young man mentioned in Mark 14:51–52. This motley crowd came in the dead of night so as not to alert the populace of Jerusalem and the surrounding area, which had swelled with visitors because of the Passover. After all, Jesus had numerous supporters and the Romans wouldn't be amused by anything that smacked of an uprising or revolt.

The people who came to arrest Jesus included Roman soldiers, the Temple guard (Jews), religious leaders, and servants of the chief priests. Matthew says they were a great multitude, possibly hundreds, armed with clubs and swords (Matthew 26:47). The face of Judas could be seen by the light of the torches and lanterns.

Following the kiss of betrayal, the sinless Son of Man was taken to trial.

## THE RELIGIOUS TRIAL

It was well past the stroke of midnight by the time Jesus faced the first of two trials, one religious and the other secular.[42] The disciples had long since fled into the night.

The powerful Sanhedrin had earlier planned to meet in the dead of night, with the goal of using the Romans to bring the death penalty on

[42] Ibid. See notation Matthew 26:57.

Christ. This entire scenario smacked of something illegal. Trials were never to be held at night and capital crimes were to be prosecuted in a public forum.[43]

The first hearing was held before Annas, the father-in-law of Caiaphas (John 18:12–14, 19–24). For a time Annas and Caiaphas shared the office of high priest (Luke 3:2 and Acts 4:6).[44] Annas had been deposed by the Romans but managed to retain his influence in an office that had morphed into a political position.[45]

Jesus was then sent for a second hearing before Caiaphas at his palace (John 18:24). According to Josephus, Caiaphas had exercised control over the high priesthood for nearly eighteen years, longer than anyone else in the first century.[46]

At the first phase of this trial, Jesus was slapped by an officer, but when he stood before the Sanhedrin, presided over by Caiaphas, his treatment was more brutal. He was blindfolded, spit upon, and slapped around by the temple guard acting on behalf of the Jewish assembly (Luke 22:52–63, Mark 15:65). Some of these guards were undoubtedly present when Judas had conferred with the chief priests in order to deliver Christ into their hands. In the English Standard Version, they're called "officers"; in the King James Version, "officers (Luke 22:3–4). These officers are often confused with Roman soldiers. Study notes in the English Standard Version point out, "Judas betrays Jesus with a kiss, and the temple guards arrest him."[47] We can be sure that all of these proceedings were carefully monitored by the Roman authorities, but at this level the Romans, including the soldiers, were little more than observers. That would soon change.

The palace of Caiaphas became a beehive of activity in the early hours of Friday morning. The curious gathered outside the compound,

---

[43] Ibid.

[44] Morris, *Henry Morris Study Bible*, 1449. See notation Matthew 26:57.

[45] *The Chronological Study Bible* (Nashville, TN: Thomas Nelson, 2008), 1229.

[46] *ESV Study Bible*, 2062. See notation John 18:24.

[47] Ibid., 1882. See notation Matthew 26:47–56.

including Peter, who had denied his Lord on three occasions. Inside, false witnesses stood before the Jewish assembly and misquoted the words of the Lord Jesus, resulting in the trumped-up charges against him. It's unlikely that all seventy members of the Sanhedrin were present at such an early hour, but the council likely included the more influential members, comprising at least the twenty-three or more required for a quorum.[48]

Following this unofficial fiasco, the Sanhedrin met again to pronounce the death penalty on Jesus. He was then bound and sent to the governor, Pontius Pilate. The religious trial was ended and the political trial would soon begin (Matthew 27:1–2).

## THE POLITICAL TRIAL

Before Matthew continues his account of the second trial, he provides some fascinating information about Judas that is found nowhere else in the other Gospels. The passion of Christ is obviously the focal point of Matthew 27.

Some have described Matthew 27:3–10 as a parenthetical to explain what happened to Judas and his thirty pieces of silver. Once this piece of information is addressed, the writer returns to the trial and suffering of the Lord Jesus. This so-called parenthetical appears to interrupt the flow of thought, but the writer obviously felt its inclusion was necessary. From this passage has arisen the tradition that Judas died before the crucifixion.

This view is not shared by all, and for good reason. Our consideration of this matter will be necessarily limited, but it makes for lively discussion. In Matthew 27, Jesus is delivered to Pilate, and Judas returns the thirty pieces of silver out of shame and remorse.

---

[48] Ibid., 1883. See notation Matthew 26:59.

## WHEN DID JUDAS DIE?

Here's what we know for certain about Judas Iscariot. He was one of the twelve apostles and is so designated in a number of passages (Matthew 26:14, 47; Mark 14:10, 43; Luke 22:47). He was the only disciple who didn't come from Galilee.[49] He was the treasurer for his fellow apostles and had a noticeable fondness for money. He then betrayed his Master for thirty pieces of silver, the going price for an injured slave (Exodus 21:32). His guilty conscience drove him to return the silver to the Jewish religious leaders, and later on he was driven to suicide by hanging, which brings us to this passage in Matthew.

Peter tells us in Acts 1:15–20 that his chosen end turned into a gory affair, which was common knowledge at the time. As he threw himself off a precipice, his body became disengaged from a rope or sash, of his own waistband, and smashed into the rocks below. One persistent tradition insists that his body was crushed under the wheels of a passing wagon, which made for a gruesome spectacle.[50] The field where Judas died was called the Field of Blood by the local population and became a place to bury the unhonoured dead. This infamous piece of real estate retained its title and intended use until the mid-1800s.[51]

Judas made his way to the Jewish leaders just as Jesus was being led out to face the governor. His sense of shame and remorse must have been almost unbearable. He most probably saw the physical signs of the brutal treatment Jesus had already received.

I wonder if they eyed each other. Matthew 27:3–10 are occupied with two major issues. The first three verses tell us what happened to Judas while the next five tell us what happened to

---

[49] Brand, ed., *The Holman Illustrated Bible Dictionary*, 959.

[50] Jimmy Swaggart, *The Expositor's Study Bible* (Baton Rouge, LA: Jimmy Swaggart Ministries, 2006), 1704. See notation 27:5.

[51] Ibid. See notation Matthew 27:8.

the thirty pieces of silver. The traditional view, held by many, is that these events happened in sequence, just as they appear in Matthew's account. Others take issue with this assessment, especially when other scriptures are taken into consideration, including 1 Corinthians 15:5, Luke 6:13–16, John 20:19–31, Mark 16:9–14, Luke 24:27–43, and Acts 1:15–26. Old Testament scriptures to be considered include Psalm 69:25, 109:8, Zechariah 11:12–13, and Jeremiah 18:1–23, 19:1–13, and 32:1–15.

These passages have often been mishandled by students of the Bible who have gone to desperate lengths to reconcile them. Taking for granted there couldn't possibly have been a time when all the apostles enumerated in Luke 6:13–16 saw Christ at one time, some have taken the number twelve to refer to the apostles generally, no matter how many of them were actually present at the time.[52] Unable to accept even the possibility that Judas could have seen the risen Christ, some have made a less than convincing attempt to squeeze Matthias into the total in 1 Corinthians 15:5.[53] Such an approach fails to note that this verse denotes a time *before* the ascension and *before* the office of Judas was filled by Matthias (Acts 1:26).

The original composition of the disciples is found in Matthew 10:1–4, as well as in Mark 3:14–18 and Luke 6:13–16. This group is repeatedly cited as the twelve throughout the Gospels and represent a full compliment of twelve people, which means Judas must be included in the total. The composition of the twelve didn't change until the death of Judas.

The evident difficulties in reconciling these accounts, including a supposed contradiction in Acts 1:18–19 when

---

[52] Robert Jamieson, A.R. Fausset, and David Brown, *Bible Commentary, Volume Three, Part Three* (Peabody, MA: Hendrickson Publishers, 2008), 327. See notation 1 Corinthians 15:5.

[53] Ibid.

compared to Matthew 27:7–10, has caused some to dismiss the passage in Acts out of hand. This is surely a slipshod approach to the Word of God that fails the test of honest exegesis. We will soon see that these verses don't present near the problem some have led us to believe.

The usual approach to this parenthetical passage in Matthew often ignores important information found in the other scriptures. Then, too, we are frequently hamstrung by tradition, which leads us to a number of false assumptions and prevents us from extracting a proper interpretation from the text.

The major emphasis in Matthew 27 is on the trials and sufferings of Messiah. The added material in Matthew 27:3–10 keeps us abreast of the movements of the betrayer during this very early morning hour. On the brink of utter despair, he is curtly dismissed by the heartless religious leaders (Matthew 27:4). According to one commentary, "A.W. Tozer calls this the great double-cross wherein Judas in collusion with the Priests betrays Christ who in turn reject him."[54] Judas throws the blood money on the marble floor of the temple with self-destruction on his mind. There is then the purchase of the potter's field, with additional details given in Acts 1.

All of this was done in fulfillment of Old Testament Scripture, but it would be a stretch to see all of this take place in the few hours during which Jesus stood before Pilate and Herod. While the writer tells us *what* happened, he fails to tell us *when* the suicide of Judas and the purchase of the field took place.

This issue was dealt with extensively by Anastasios Kioulachoglou in the *Journal of Biblical Accuracy* in 1996, and it was reprinted in *Baptist Magazine* two years later. The writer presents two major arguments to support his conviction that Judas was still

[54] *Liberty Bible Commentary* (Lynchburg, VA: The Old Time Gospel Hour, 1983), 1957. See notation Matthew 27:3–8.

alive following the resurrection. The first is the clear statement of 1 Corinthians 15:5 that he was *"then of the twelve"* (KJV).[55] Kioulachoglou concluded that

> the time of Judas' death might have minor significance if we didn't have problems with the accuracy of the Word of God… then the examination is no longer a simple examination of the time that Judas died but an examination of the accuracy of the Word of God…[56]
>
> Those that have any idea of the time that is usually needed to only find the appropriate property know that this requires several days, weeks and sometimes months. If we were to read this parenthetical passage as many of us read the one that precedes it about Judas. i.e. by taking everything in a time sequence, then we would conclude that while Jesus was before the governor (verses 1–2) Judas returned the money and hanged himself, the priests took the money, consulted together, found someone that was selling a field, saw the field, reached an agreement about it and made the contracts. All these are simply impossible to happen when Jesus was standing before the governor, and in fact, without any progress in his investigation. Moreover, an interpretation like this would contradict all that we have seen from the other Gospels and from 1 Corinthians that suggest that Judas was alive after the resurrection.[57]

The chief priests and elders who comprised the powerful Sanhedrin had just condemned Jesus to death and sent him for trial before the Roman authorities. They had been planning

[55] Anastasios Kioulachoglou, "Judas: When Did He Die?" *Baptist Magazine*, January–February 1998, 19–21.

[56] Ibid., 31–32.

[57] Ibid., 27.

for many months to use every means available to bring about the death of Christ, and their objective was within reach in the early hours of Good Friday.

They rushed Judas out of their presence, not caring if he lived or died. They had no time to concern themselves with his possible suicide or to leave the temple compound in order to buy the field where he would so tragically die. They had no idea what Judas' intentions were when he left their presence—and they didn't care.

These events transpired in fulfillment of the OT Scriptures, but not on the same day. The priests and elders probably stayed up all night in order to push their wicked agenda. To leave the city right then would have been unthinkable. Besides, no scriptures prove conclusively that Judas died prior to the crucifixion of Christ.

Three of the four Gospels record the appearance of the resurrected Christ on the evening of the first day of the week (Mark 16:14, Luke 24:33, John 20:19). This is the same day He arose from the dead. Jesus appeared to His disciples in John 20:19. John doesn't specifically state who was present, but we learn from John 20:24 that Thomas was not there.

This same appearance is recorded in the last chapter of Luke. Not only are these appearances similar, they are identical. The two individuals who met the risen Christ on the road to Emmaus returned to Jerusalem where they found *"the eleven gathered together"* (Luke 24:33, KJV).

Tradition tells us that the missing disciple is Judas, who is presumably already dead by this time. But is that assumption correct? We know from John's Gospel that Thomas wasn't present on this occasion, leaving eleven disciples, not ten, as we might expect. This can only mean that Judas is still alive.

Mark's Gospel repeats what we have seen in both John and Luke. Mark 16:14 says, *"Afterward he appeared unto the eleven as they sat at meat...*" (KJV) It surely must be evident that eleven means eleven, unless we would be so bold as to question the accuracy of the Bible in three different Gospels that speak of the same occasion. Or did Thomas find his way in while we weren't looking?

There is an interesting observation in James White's discussion of the various endings of Mark 16. White takes notice that there appears to be a problem with the number eleven in Mark 16:14. Though the discussion here has nothing to do with the timing of Judas' passing, but rather with the validity of the longer ending of Mark, it's interesting that White seems to use this as an argument against the longer ending.

I would contend that whether Mark 16:14 is part of the original text, the issue has nothing to do with the number of disciples present. This only presents a problem if we assume that Judas is already dead. The fact remains that Mark's account is in full agreement with the other Gospels. Taking the Gospel accounts as they stand, with or without the additional information in 1 Corinthians 15:5, we can come to only one conclusion: Judas bore witness to the resurrected Christ. Here is White's observation:

> The second problem crops up in verse 14 [of Mark 16], where we have eleven disciples at the table. Aside from the possible numerical problem (was not Thomas absent?), here we are told that "Jesus reproached them for their unbelief and hardness of heart.[58]

We are still looking for the twelve spoken of in 1 Corinthians 15:5, the resurrection chapter. It would be unrealistic to look for a verse to match every post-resurrection appearance, but if twelve

---

[58] James R. White, *The King James Only Controversy* (Minneapolis, MN: Bethany House, 2009), 319.

means twelve, the answer can be found in a return visit to John's Gospel: *"But Thomas, one of the twelve, called Didymus was not with them when Jesus came"* (John 20:24, KJV) The reference here to "them" must surely refer to the disciples who were gathered together on the evening of the first day of the week (John 20:19), an occasion at which Thomas was not present. He refused to accept the word of his fellow disciples, insisting on visible, tangible evidence: *"And after eight days again his disciples were within, and Thomas with them: then came Jesus, the doors being shut, and stood in the midst, and said, Peace be unto you"* (John 20:26, KJV).

The last I heard, eleven plus one equals twelve, which has a familiar ring to 1 Corinthians 15:5.

The only way to disprove the possibility that Judas died after the resurrection, rather than before the crucifixion, is to approach Matthew 27:3–5 with a preconceived notion that the events in this passage, including the appearance of Christ before the governor in Matthew 27:11, happened in this exact sequence, with no time lapse. We must also ignore all the other scriptures that would tend to disprove this rather untenable theory.

Some will question whether any of this matters one way or the other. It does matter that we allow Scripture to speak for itself rather than being hamstrung with questionable assumptions.

An examination of commentaries and study Bibles reveals some interesting approaches to 1 Corinthians 15:5. There seems to be a determination to ignore its implications. The notation in the Scofield Reference Bible is somewhat ponderous. We are taken to Mark 16:14 and a brief comment: "A collective term equivalent to 'The Sanhedrin,' 'The Commons' not necessarily implying that eleven persons were present. See Lk. 24:33; 1 Cor. 15:5; and cf. Mt. 28:16 where 'eleven disciples' implies a definite number of persons."[59] I hardly find this helpful to the serious Bible student.

---

[59] *The Scofield Reference Bible* (New York, NY: Oxford University Press, 1917), 1069.

A comment from the much-respected Matthew Henry's commentary is equally as puzzling: "He was seen of Cephas, or Peter, then of the twelve, called so, though Judas was no longer among them because this was their usual number…"[60]

The ESV Study Bible says that the twelve includes Matthias, but I find this untenable.[61] The Geneva Bible of 1599 states, "Of those twelve picked and chosen Apostles, which were commonly called twelve, though Judas was put out of the number."[62] The *New Bible Commentary* offers no comment,[63] and neither does the Liberty Bible Commentary.[64] Harry Ironside's commentary is also silent.[65]

What we do know is that sometime during the forty-day post-resurrection ministry of Christ, and before the ascension in Acts 1, a despondent and guilt-ridden Judas made his lonely trek to the Valley of Hinnom, which lay south of Jerusalem.[66] It was here that the man, whose name is synonymous with deceit and betrayal, met his violent end. It is no accident that parents never consider Judas as a possible name for their sons.

We now connect the dots, proving once again the unique character of God's Word, the Bible. The field of blood mentioned in Acts 1:19 has traditionally been identified as the Valley of Hinnom for two thousand years.[67] A careful reading of Jeremiah 18–19 will place the potter's house in the Valley of Hinnom.

We must not miss the fascinating analogy in Jeremiah 32:7–10, where Jeremiah purchases a field in Anathoth. This

---

[60] Matthew Henry, *Matthew Henry's Commentary* (Peabody, MA: Hendrickson Publishers, 1991), 472.

[61] *ESV Study Bible*, 2213. See notation 1 Corinthians 15:5.

[62] *The 1599 Geneva Bible* (White Hall, WV: Tolle Press, 2006–2007), 1185.

[63] *New Bible Commentary* (Downers Grove, IL: IVP Academic, 2007), 1183.

[64] *Liberty Bible Commentary*, 2326.

[65] H.A. Ironside, *1 Corinthians* (Neptune, NJ: Loizeaux Brothers, 1938), 465.

[66] *The New Bible Dictionary*, 475.

[67] Merrill F. Unger, *Unger's Bible Dictionary* (Chicago, IL: Moody Press, 1971), 16.

purchase has huge implications, since it transpired while the Babylonians were very nearly storming the gates of the city they were destined to destroy. This transaction was an act of faith on the part of Jeremiah, who believed that at a future time the Jews would return to their land and rebuild their beloved city of Jerusalem. This took place decades later, following the decree of Cyrus that permitted the Jews to return to their land.

An interesting comparison can be made with the potter's field (Matthew 27:7–10), which in Luke's rendition is called Aceldama (Hakeldama) or the field of blood. The potter's field was purchased by the Sanhedrin while the land was occupied by the Roman army.

Pulling all these Scriptures together, we will now consider the location where Judas Iscariot died.

Bible scholars are now largely convinced that the potter's field and the field of blood are one and the same and located in what the Old Testament calls the Valley of Hinnom.[68]

This valley has some notable features. In this desolate place, little babies were laid in the arms of Molech, where they were burned to death in a blazing inferno. This idolatrous Canaanitish practice sometimes attracted Jewish adherents during times of apostasy.[69] First noted in Leviticus 18:21, this ritual continued until after the ministry of Jeremiah.[70] Refuse of all kinds was incinerated almost non-stop in this valley. Operating like a gigantic crematorium, the Valley of Hinnom became the final depository for the corpses of animals and criminals alike.[71] The soil in this area was excellent for pottery making.

---

[68] *ESV Study Bible*, 1884.

[69] *Liberty Bible Commentary*, 1460.

[70] *The Apologetics Study Bible* (Nashville, TN: Holman Publishers, 2007), 179.

[71] Unger, *Unger's Bible Dictionary*, 484.

This virtual valley of death with its storied history of morbidity became the final resting place of Judas Iscariot.[72]

The betrayer of Christ was no more guilty than the men who had paid him for his foul deed. He had walked with Christ for over three years and was counted among the twelve apostles. His return of the paltry sum of thirty pieces of silver to the blind and hardened religious leaders shows at least some measure of remorse, if not true repentance.

Bible students, scholars, and translators continue to mull over the proper exegesis of Matthew 27:3. Perhaps the sight of his disemboweled and rotting corpse spurred the Jewish elite in Jerusalem to purchase for posterity the field in which Judas died. Acting on behalf of their fellow conspirator, the best-known traitor in history, they struck a deal for the potter's field, and in doing so they fulfilled the Scriptures they had long ago abandoned (Zechariah 11:12–13, Matthew 15:1–3).

The reference to Jeremiah in Matthew 27:9 has been puzzling to some, since these details are nowhere to be found in Jeremiah. Commentators offer a number of explanations. Quite possibly, Jeremiah is used in a general way to represent all Old Testament prophets.[73] Another possibility is that this statement may have been said by Jeremiah but never written down.[74]

H.A. Ironside offers yet another option: "J.N. Darby suggests that the book of Zechariah formed part of a scroll which began with the prophecy of Jeremiah, and therefore would bear his name; and so it could be spoken of as an utterance found in 'Jeremiah.'"[75]

---

[72] Brand, ed., *The Holman Illustrated Bible Dictionary*, 765.

[73] *ESV Study Bible*, 1884. See notation Matthew 27:9–10.

[74] Morris, *Henry Morris Study Bible*, 1451.

[75] H.A. Ironside, *Matthew* (Neptune, NJ: Loizeaux Brothers, 1948), 375.

Additional material concerning the place of the death of Judas is found in the notes of Albert Barnes.[76] Another excellent resource is *the Zondervan Encyclopedia of the Bible.*[77]

Whether the Jewish establishment realized it or not, they were largely responsible for the deaths of both Christ (1 Corinthians 2:8) and His betrayer. They adroitly engineered the murder of Jesus, then abandoned Judas to his own destruction (Matthew 27:4).

The first appearance of Jesus before Pilate (Matthew 27:2–11, Luke 23:1–5) was of short duration. His audience with Herod is recorded only by Luke and isn't noted by the other Gospel writers (Luke 23:6–12). Herod was the governor of Galilee and had his principle residence in Capernaum, which was the headquarters of Christ.

Perhaps Pilate was seeking encouragement from his rival ruler, with whom he was usually at odds (Luke 23:12). It's not known what his primary motive was in sending Jesus to Herod, who was in Jerusalem for Passover. Known to history as Herod Antipas, Herod was responsible for the imprisonment and execution of John the Baptist (Matthew 14:1–12).

Herod was met by an entourage of chief priests and scribes who continued their attacks on Jesus. Herod could find no reason to condemn Christ, but he and his men used the opportunity to make sport with Jesus for the sheer delight of those present. His many trivial questions and pompous mannerisms produced only silence from Jesus, who was sent back to Pilate for what would be His final hearing.

Perhaps Pilate had hoped Herod would assume responsibility for this protracted trial, which was fueled by Jewish antagonism toward

[76] Albert Barnes, *Barne's Notes* (Grand Rapids, MI: Baker Book, 2005), 300–301.

[77] *The Zondervan Encyclopedia of the Bible* (Grand Rapids, MI: Akeldama, 2009), 108–109.

Jesus, but history dictated otherwise. John records the lively exchange that ensued between Pilate and Christ, especially concerning truth and authority (John 18:33–38, Matthew 27:11–14).

Following this private conversation in Pilate's own residence (John 18:33), Jesus was again brought out to face the Jewish leaders. Pilate was in a desperate dilemma. He found Jesus innocent but feverishly laboured to appease the people. He was in a no-win situation. Roman custom dictated that a prisoner of the people's choosing could be released each year at Passover, and on this occasion Barabbas was chosen to be freed. An interesting tradition suggests Barabbas' first name was Jesus.[78] In Aramaic, Barabbas means "the father's son," in contrast with Jesus, which means "the Father's son."[79]

The people then demanded that Jesus of Nazareth be crucified (Matthew 27:15–26). During this emotional firestorm, Pilate received a message from his wife, Claudia Procula (Matthew 27:19).[80] She had awakened from a disturbing dream and warned her husband to have no part in condemning Jesus. Only Matthew records this incident. Indeed, Claudia was the only person to say a kind word about Jesus during His trial. Tradition says that she became a genuine believer at a later time.[81]

The Romans had executed many thousands of prisoners by crucifixion, an ancient craft they had finetuned during their years of domination and empire. With Christ found guilty by His own people, Pilate found himself pulled into an inescapable decision. Worn out from the pressure, he turned Jesus over to strong and cruel soldiers who carried out the sentence of death with acute and painful precision.

Unknown to the rabble who had rejected their Messiah, and the Romans who had been manipulated to do their bidding, the death of Christ would fulfill many hundreds of Old Testament prophecies.

---

[78] Ibid., 504.

[79] *Liberty Bible Commentary*, 1957.

[80] Dr. Herbert Lockyer, *The Women of the Bible* (Grand Rapids, MI: Zondervan, 1974), 226–227.

[81] Swaggart, *The Expositor's Study Bible*, 1705. See notation Matthew 27:19.

Perhaps the most graphic description of the crucifixion had been given centuries before the horrible practice had even come into popular use. This is found in Isaiah 53. Those reading Scripture in the time of Isaiah would have been puzzled by the description.

Roman crucifixion was preceded by a vicious beating that often killed the victim before crucifixion could be enacted. Matthew 27:26 informs us that this was administered to Christ as soon as Barabbas was released.

After being cruelly mocked and continually beaten, Christ was led out to Golgotha to be crucified. Simon of Cyrene was selected from the crowd of onlookers to carry His cross. This was a common practice, as many victims were simply too weak. While Christ lived only six hours on the cross, some lived many more hours and even days before succumbing to the inevitable.

Matthew then relates how the veil of the temple, made of woven leather and three inches thick, ripped from top to bottom when Jesus expired (Matthew 27:50–51). This massive curtain blocked the entrance to the Most Holy Place.[82]

## EMPTY TOMBS

Matthew is the only writer to report the presence of resurrected saints in the Jerusalem following the resurrection of Christ (Matthew 27:52–53). This incident didn't take place until Christ had risen from the grave, but it's reported in Matthew's writings in the context of the crucifixion three days earlier.

This is one of those many instances when God goes right outside the box of what many expect Him to do. The usual workings of God are sometimes interrupted by what seems to us to be unusual. He is a sovereign God who likes to delight us with the unexpected.

Matthew's description is very explicit. These saints were raised bodily from the dead and their number is not given. These saints lived and died prior to the resurrection of Christ. John MacArthur says,

---

[82] Ibid., 1707. See notation Matthew 27:50–51.

"Evidently, these people were given glorified bodies; they appeared to many (vs. 53) enough to establish the reality of the miracle; and then they no doubt ascended to glory- a kind of foretaste of 1 Thessalonians 4:16."[83] This passage needs little explanation and should be received exactly as given, without undue speculation.

The final five verses of Matthew 27 give us a sense of the paranoia that existed among the chief priests and Pharisees following the crucifixion. As they assembled before Pilate, they recalled the words of Christ concerning His resurrection on the third day. This meeting took place on the Sabbath and they requested that two precautions be taken regarding the tomb: it was to be sealed and guarded to discount any possibility of the body being stolen, thus sparking false rumors about a possible resurrection. The seal consisted of a cord around the stone and secured at each end with wax or clay. The stone could not be moved without the seal being broken. Pilate granted their requests, including a guard to watch the tomb (Matthew 27:66).

The final chapter of Matthew records that the tomb was found empty when investigated early Sunday morning by Mary Magdalene and the other Mary.

From Matthew 28:11–15, as we read of the bribery of the soldiers, we witness a glaring contradiction—not of the Scriptures, but of the customs and practice of the day. In the time of Christ, Roman soldiers who allowed their prisoners to escape were summoned to a speedy execution by their superiors. According to the Scriptures, some of the soldiers who stood watch over the tomb of Christ made their way to the chief priests where they accepted a bribe to lie about the events of that early morning. Incredibly, they were instructed to admit to having fallen asleep and allowing the disciples of Christ to steal His body. If they had been sleeping, how would they have known who stole His body?

The truth is found in Matthew 28:4, where we see the guards so stricken with fear that they were unable to move as they gazed upon the angel who had rolled away the stone. Jesus had already risen and left

[83] MacArthur, *The MacArthur Study Bible*, 1449–1450.

the tomb. The stone wasn't moved to let Jesus out but to let the people in so they could witness that Christ had risen.

There has been much discussion about the tightened security around the grave. Many of us assume that a small contingent of Roman soldiers was assigned the task, but not all commentators are agreed. Guard duty among Roman soldiers was taken very seriously by their superiors and breaches of trust were usually met with immediate execution. This is well illustrated by Peter's miraculous escape from prison in Acts 12. He was bound to two Roman soldiers while he slept, while at least eight more guarded the door (Acts 12:4, 6–10). Herod's response to Peter's escape was to order the execution of all the guards (Acts 12:18–19).

Some commentators have capably argued that the soldiers assigned to secure the tomb of Christ weren't under the employ of Rome, but rather part of the Jewish militia, charged with guarding the temple precinct against vandalism. History appears to support the assumption that Rome permitted a limited number of Jewish soldiers to be retained by the priests for the protection of the temple. It was a way for Rome to foster goodwill with her subjects. These lightly armed security guards posed no threat to the strong Roman presence in the city. I'm personally attracted to this possibility, especially seen against the backdrop of the concocted story put together by the authorities following the resurrection.

Pilate had better things to do than to have his crack troops stand guard over a cemetery. The words of the governor in Matthew 27:65, *"Ye have a watch"* (KJV), could refer to the men who were normally employed in temple duty.

*The Apologetics Study Bible* leaves the issue open: "It is difficult to tell whether the guards mentioned here were Roman troops or Jewish temple guards. Pilate's words may imply either."[84] From *The New Bible Dictionary* comes this interesting comment:

> The Temple had its own police department known as the Temple Guard, who were mostly Levites and whose task, among other

[84] *The Apologetics Study Bible*, 1460. See notation Matthew 28:11.

> things, was to keep out the forbidden Gentiles (cf. Mt. 27:65, RSV) The spekoulator, a Latinism found in Mk. 6:27, was one of ten such officers attached to a legion who acted mostly as couriers but sometimes as executioners: one such was in the employ of Herod Antipos.[85]

Note the wording of Matthew 27:65 from the RSV: *"Pilate said to them, 'You have a guard of soldiers: go, make it as secure as you can.'"* The ESV has the exact same reading.

Frank Morison, the pen name for Albert Henry Ross, seems to offer the most practical solution to what appears to some as a problem in Matthew 27:62–66. The answer is found in the biblical account. The Pharisees approached Pilate with a request that was laughable at best: to place a guard at the tomb as a precautionary measure. Pilate's terse response is a firm refusal, probably because it seemed so ridiculous and unnecessary.

In keeping with his character, Pilate washed his hands of the whole business in the same way he had removed himself from complicity in the condemnation of Christ. I wonder if he literally washed his hands a second time (Matthew 27:24).

This small contingent of guards was drawn from the temple police and responsible only to Caiaphas and the Jewish authorities who had requested their services. From Matthew 28:11–15, we learn that they were financially rewarded and promised full protection.

If they are seen as a Roman detachment set by Pilate himself and under the command of a centurion, there is a difficulty here. Morison aptly reminds us that the procuring of the guard, designed to keep the tomb from being violated, had just the opposite effect. The guards, rather than falling asleep as falsely claimed by them, were wide awake at the tomb, and thus they became unlikely witnesses to the resurrection of Christ.[86]

---

85 *The New Bible Dictionary*, 437.

86 Frank Morison, *Who Moved the Stone?* (Grand Rapids, MI: Zondervan, 2002), 158–190.

Further light is added by Matthew Henry. We return to Pilate's words in Matthew 27:65, *"Ye have a watch: go your way, make it as sure as ye can"* (KJV):

> He [Pilate] was ready to gratify Christ's friends, in allowing them the body, and his enemies, in setting a guard upon it, being desirous to please all sides, while perhaps he laughed in his sleeve at both for making such ado, pro and con, about the hopes of one side and the fears of the other to be alike ridiculous. Ye have a watch; he means the constant guard that was kept in the tower of Antonia, out of which he allows them to detach as many as they please for that purpose, but, as if ashamed to be himself seen in such a thing, he leaves the management of it wholly to them.[87]

The tower of Antonia was built as a fortress around AD 6 and was named for Mark Antony, friend of Herod the Great. The tower was built at the northwest corner of the temple and served as a barracks for troops as well as a depository for the vestments of the high priest. This structure was destroyed by Titus in AD 66.[88]

The seal affixed to the stone of the tomb was probably that of the Sanhedrin, which combined with the watchers (guards) was designed to keep out intruders and keep Christ in the grave. Perhaps Pilate himself knew their efforts were futile, especially if he had spoken with the centurion who upon witnessing the moving of the rocks and the earthquake openly acknowledged that Jesus was the Son of God (Matthew 27:54). Not wanting to be part of a failed enterprise, he wisely removed himself from the situation while giving the religious leaders what they wanted.

A shrewd politician, Pilate gave them the men what they wanted and may have even been under conviction, but like Agrippa and Felix

---

[87] Matthew Henry, *Matthew Henry's Commentary* (Peabody, MA: Hendrickson Publishers, 1991), 353–354.

[88] Brand, ed., *The Holman Illustrated Bible Dictionary*, 77–78.

at a later time he never became fully persuaded of the claims of Christ in the grave.

> So they intended, but God brought this good out of it, that they who were set to oppose his resurrection, thereby had an opportunity to observe it, and did so, and told the chief priests what they observed, who were thereby rendered the more inexcusable. Here was all the power of earth and hell combined to keep Christ a prisoner, but all in vain.[89]

Should this be the correct interpretation of events, it would mean that the devious cover-up was solely of Jewish origin, with no collusion from the Roman military. Whatever the makeup of the men given guard duty over the burial place of Jesus, they were bribed by the Sanhedrin to tell the most incredible story of the disciples stealing the body of Jesus while they slept. The story was still being repeated and embraced in the second century during the days of Justin Martyr.[90]

## THE GREAT COMMISSION

Matthew closes with what is now referred to as the Great Commission. In reference to this command to go and make disciples and to baptize them in the name of the Father, and of the Son, and of the Holy Spirit, here are some excellent comments from the pen of Dr. R. Barry Beebe. Dr. Beebe is the former president of the New Brunswick Bible Institute in Victoria Corner, New Brunswick:

- Have you and your spouse committed your lives to the Great Commission of our Lord Jesus Christ? Is your life dedicated to glorifying God by evangelism and discipleship?

---

[89] Henry, *Matthew Henry's Commentary*, 354.

[90] *New Geneva Study Bible* (Nashville, TN: Thomas Nelson, 1995), 1555–1556. See notation Matthew 28:11–15.

- Are you raising your children and grandchildren to consider a life on the mission field; to be open to God's call to full-time Christian work; to value the privilege of devoting one's life to the proclamation of the Gospel?
- Do your children and grandchildren know that you pray for missionaries, give to support missionaries, entertain traveling missionaries and are involved in your local church's missions program and missionary meetings?
- Have you gone or have you encouraged your children or grandchildren to go on short-term mission trips?

We are far behind in our task of getting the Gospel to the world in each generation. There are often more missionaries coming home than going forth.

Why have we made secular work, secure careers, university education, high salaries, good benefits, comfortable retirement and the accumulation of this world's goods so important to our children and grandchildren? What about a life of faith, a life of service, a life of sacrifice, a life devoted to the call of Jesus?

Do our children and grandchildren see our homes as missionary homes and do they see our lives devoted to the Great Commission?[91]

[91] Dr. Barry Beebe, "The President's Challenge," *Open Bible Bulletin* (Victoria Corner, NB: New Brunswick Bible Institute, February 2010).

# The Gospel According to Mark

In the book of Acts, the author of this Gospel is revealed to be named John, although his surname was Mark (Acts 12:12, 25; 15:37, 39). Mark's name is derived from the Latin name Marcus and means "large hammer." From the earliest days of church history, Mark has been considered the author of the book that bears his name.

There are sixteen chapters in Mark's Gospel broken into:

- The Ministry of John the Baptist (1:1–11)
- Healings and the Sabbath Controversy (1:12–3:12)
- Four Parables and the Sea Stilled (4:1–41)
- Dealing with Demons and the Healing of Jairus' Daughter (5:1–43)
- John the Baptist is Murdered, Jesus Walks on the Water (6:1–56)
- The Pharisees and Defilement (7:1–23)
- Miracles of Healing and Provision (8:1–38)
- The Transfiguration (9:1–13)
- Demon Possession and Warnings about Hell (9:14–50)

- Marriage and Divorce (10:1–16)
- The Problem with Riches and the Coming Crucifixion (10:17–52)
- The Triumphal Entry (11:1–14)
- Faith, Forgiveness and Authority (11:15–33)
- Parable of the Vineyard (12:1–12)
- Jesus Debates with the Leaders (12:13–44)
- Global Turmoil and the Second Coming (13:1–27)
- The Fig Tree and the Exhortation to Watch (13:28–37)
- The Plot to Kill Jesus and His Anointing (14:1–11)
- The Passover, the Lord's Supper, and Gethsemane (14:17–42)
- Betrayal, Trial and Denial (14:43–72)
- The Crucifixion (15:1–47)
- The Resurrection (16:1–20_

## SUMMARY

The Gospel of Mark is the shortest of the synoptic Gospels and shorter than the Gospel of John. Early church writers are agreed that John Mark was a close companion of the Apostle Peter and that much of his Gospel material was taken from Peter's preaching and ministry.

When Peter was released from prison, as recorded in Acts 12, he found refuge at the home of John Mark's mother in Jerusalem (Acts 12:12). Some have noted that Mark is careful to reference the weakness of Peter as well as those of other apostles. Others have observed striking similarities between Peter's speech in Caesarea and the Gospel of Mark.[92]

Unlike Matthew, who accents the kingly role of Christ, Mark emphasizes the servanthood of Christ. Skipping many of the lengthy discourses found in the other Gospels, Mark pays special attention to deeds of service and sacrifice. More than any of the other evangelists, Mark demonstrates the human qualities of Christ, especially His human

---

[92] Paul Barnett, *The Birth of Christianity: The First Twenty Years* (Grand Rapids, MI: William E. Eerdmans Publishing, 2005), 160–162.

emotions and limitations. The universal call of Jesus to discipleship is thematic in the second Gospel, and that call is connected to a vital and ongoing relationship with the Lord Jesus Christ. The discipleship Mark represents is far more than a certain code of conduct or adherence to rules and regulations; it is a deep and abiding fellowship that embraces all that Christ stands for, trusting Him explicitly, serving Him faithfully, and, if called upon, facing the kind of rejection Christ Himself faced during His shortened life on our sin-cursed planet.

Mark's Gospel targeted a largely Gentile audience outside of Palestine, people who were unfamiliar with Jewish customs and practices. Those same societal behaviours are carefully explained to his readers in order to help them grasp the meaning of the coming of Christ as the culmination of God's work with the nation of Israel and the remainder of humanity.

There is a fast-paced element in Mark's Gospel as he moves quickly from one stirring event to the next, like a modern-day reporter gathering information for the evening newscast. He used the word *immediately* more than forty times, which is not always apparent in the King James Version where words like anon, forthwith, and straightaway are all used in place of the same Greek word for immediacy. Mark is a man of action who is far more concerned with what Jesus did than with what He said.

Mark's opening line—*"The beginning of the Gospel of Jesus Christ, the Son of God"* (Mark 1:1, KJV)—is generally accepted as the title for his Gospel, and in it the writer gets right to his subject. He doesn't begin his Gospel with an elaborate preface but rather tells us his subject: the good news about Jesus the Christ (or Messiah).[93]

Moving at lightning speed, and taking no time for the genealogies and nativity scenes that are given in vivid detail in Matthew and Luke, Mark takes us, in just thirteen verses, from John the Baptist's ministry in the wilderness to the temptation of Christ. He skips the drama and ensuing conversation between Christ and Satan recorded

---

[93] *The New Bible Commentary*, 950.

in other accounts, going directly to the preaching ministry of Christ in Galilee, which results in the calling of the first disciples and the healing of multitudes, including the healing of Peter's mother-in-law and the leper, with which Mark 1 ends.

By the time we get to the end of Mark 3, there is already growing controversy over the Sabbath as well as a plot by the Herodions and Pharisees to murder Christ. Mark records the selection of the twelve (Mark 3:13–19).

Four parables, including that of the soils, are recorded in Mark 4 as well as the stilling of the sea. In the next chapter, we see the demon entering into the swine, as well as the healing of Jairus' daughter.

From Mark 6:3, we learn that Christ was one of at least seven children. His half-brothers were James, Joses, Judas, and Simon, along with at least two half-sisters who remain unnamed. In this same chapter, Mark devotes sixteen verses to the gruesome details of the murder of John the Baptist, whose severed head was delivered on a platter to a dance floor to satisfy the hatred of Herod's wife (Mark 6:28).

The first twenty-three verses of Mark 7 deal with the subject of defilement and details how tradition can easily displace the commands of God. The better part of this passage deals with the cost of discipleship.

The transfiguration is seen in Mark 9, and in the following chapter there is a spirited debate about marriage and divorce. The triumphal entry, which is celebrated each year on our calendar as Palm Sunday, is detailed in Mark 11. The next chapter includes a lively discussion between Christ and the Sadducees about the resurrection of the body, a teaching that wasn't embraced by this Jewish religious sect.

Mark 13 is a shortened version of Matthew 24 as Christ predicts the future destruction of the temple and the devastation of the city. Mark 14:1–15:47 recounts all the events leading up to and including the crucifixion.

The mysterious young man clad only in his bedclothes who shows up in Mark 14:51–52 has prompted endless discussion as to his identity and possible motive for being there. His attempt to follow

Jesus was abruptly halted when he was accosted by a not so friendly mob. He lost his linen cloth in the scuffle and was forced to flee naked into the darkness of the night. This incident is recorded only by Mark, suggesting that he himself may have been the man in question.[94]

## A CONTESTED CONCLUSION

The last chapter of Mark is occupied with the resurrection of Christ, a passage that has prompted endless discussion. Some of the earlier Greek manuscripts do not include Mark 16:9–20. Some later documents not only include these verses but add another paragraph to the chapter. In some of the manuscripts, these words are sandwiched between Mark 16:8–9. Some records of Mark's Gospel also add an "Amen" to end the chapter.

How do we account for these discrepancies, and which documents can we trust? A great deal of research has gone into this issue and the debate has continued since the days of the early church.

The New American Standard Bible adds the aforementioned paragraph to the longer ending of Mark, but since those words are of more recent origin in some of the more recent translations I am inclined to ignore them—for two reasons: firstly, there seems not to be enough evidence to include them, and secondly, I find the words to be wooden and lifeless; they appear to be out of character with not only Mark's Gospel but the others as well.

We note, too, that they are placed in italics, which indicates a high degree of unreliability. Without passing judgment on others of a different persuasion, the words are given here for your personal appraisal: *"And they promptly reported all these instructions to Peter and his companions. And after that, Jesus*

---

[94] *New American Standard Bible, Key Word Study Bible* (La Habra, CA: The Lockman Foundation, 1995), 1312.

*Himself sent out through them from east to west the sacred and imperishable proclamation of eternal salvation"* (Mark 16:20, NASB).

We are now left with the two remaining options for the last chapter of Mark. There is the standard longer ending that is found in almost every English translation, including the familiar King James Version. The New King James Version embraces the longer ending by placing an Amen at the end; this is found in some older documents which I think provides an appropriate conclusion to the Gospel.

Some translations come with the shorter ending, ending the chapter at Mark 16:8, which is supported by some manuscripts. It is to be noted that these same versions usually include the longer ending as a separate notation or as a footnote at the bottom of the page. Such is the case with the Revised Standard Version of 1952 and the American Standard Version of 1901.

The ESV Study Bible wisely includes both endings, noting that Mark 16:9–20 are absent in some manuscripts. The notes in this Bible tell us that most of the material in these verses is present in other New Testament passages. Caution should be taken: "With particular reference to v. 18, there is no command to pick up serpents or to drink deadly poison; there is merely a promise of protection as found in other parts of the NT (Acts 28:3–4; James 5:13–16)."[95]

[95] *ESV Study Bible*, 1933. See notation Mark 16:9–20.

# The Gospel According to Luke

**As is the case with the other three Gospels, the title of the one is derived** from the name of the author. Very little is known about the third Gospel writer, but early tradition seems to point to his being from the city of Antioch. According to Colossians 4:11–14, he was a Gentile convert who is referred to as a beloved physician. He's the only Gentile writer of either testament and we are indebted to him for not one but two books, as he is also credited as the author of the book of Acts.

Luke was a traveling companion to the Apostle Paul following the Macedonian vision in Acts 16. His medical background can be seen in his description of various maladies, which becomes especially evident in his Gospel. Luke's unique style of Greek writing and his beauty of presentation suggests that he was the most cultured and perhaps best educated of the Gospel writers.[96]

There are twenty-four chapters in Luke's Gospel broken into:

---

[96] *New American Standard Bible, Key Word Study Bible* (Chattanooga, TN: AMG Publishers, 1977), 1343.

- The Introduction (1:1–4)
- John the Baptist (1:5–25, 57–80)
- Mary and Elisabeth (1:26–56)
- Christ: Birth and Boyhood (2:1–52)
- The Preaching of John the Baptist (3:1–22)
- Genealogy of Jesus (3:23–38)
- Jesus: Temptation and Public Ministry (4:1–44)
- The First Disciples (5:1–39)
- The Sabbath and the Calling of the Twelve (6:1–19)
- The Beatitudes (6:20–49)
- Healing Ministry (7:1–17)
- John the Baptist and Jesus (7:18–39)
- Parable of Two Debtors (7:40–50)
- Parables, Miracles and the Stilling of the Sea (8:1–56)
- The Transfiguration and the Test of Greatness (9:1–62)
- The Seventy (10:1–42)
- Prayer (11:1–13)
- The Pharisees (11:14–54)
- Seek First the Kingdom of God (12:1–59)
- Suffering and Healing (13:1–17)
- Parables and Teaching (13:18–35)
- Discipleship Tested (14:1–35)
- The Lost Sheep, the Lost Coin, and the Prodigal Son (15:1–32)
- The Unjust Employer (16:1–18)
- The Rich Man and Lazarus (16:19–31)
- Increase Our Faith (17:1–37)
- Prayer and the Young Ruler (18:1–43)
- Zacharias, Money, and the Triumphal Entry (19:1–48)
- Authority and Tribute (20:1–47)
- Future Events (21:1–38)
- The Passover and Gethsemane (22:1–71)
- The Crucifixion (23:1–56)
- The Resurrection (24:1–53)

## SUMMARY

The single-sentence prologue that takes up the first four verses of Luke's Gospel is presented in a polished Greek style that ranks among the finest of first-century writing. Giving full credit to his sources, Luke gathers his material in an orderly fashion and addresses his Gospel to the most excellent Theophilus, suggesting that he was a governor or other dignitary of the highest order.

> Until recently, theologians thought that Theophilus was a representative member of the Roman Government or that the name "Theophilus" meaning "Dear to God" was a pseudonym for a Gentile Official who Luke desired to see the Gospel more favorably. Yet, as supported by Josephus… and as seen in our archeological evidence found among the Herodian Mansions in the Jewish Quarter of Jerusalem, Theophilus was the high priest between 37–41 CE. This is significant in that Luke begins and ends this Gospel account with references to the Temple.[97]

Additional information comes to us from Merrill F. Unger's Bible Dictionary: "Theophilus, the son of Ananus, was the high priest from whom Saul received letters to the synagogue of Damascus (Acts 9:1, 14)."[98]

Luke addresses both his biography of Christ, in his Gospel, and his history of the church's first thirty years, in Acts, to the former high priest whom he calls the most honourable Theophilus (Luke 1:3, Acts 1:1). For reasons unknown, but perhaps out of respect or to guard against any embarrassment to a respected official, Luke chooses not to include the name of Theophilus in Acts 9:1. It becomes clear that Luke is motivated in his writings to either win the former high priest to the Christian faith or to further encourage him in his walk with Christ. Luke became a close friend and co-labourer with the Apostle

[97] *The Complete Jewish Study Bible* (Peabody, MA: Hendrickson Publishers, 2016), 1469.
[98] Unger, *Unger's Bible Dictionary*, 889.

Paul, and so it appears he also befriended the same high priest who had authorized Paul to wreak havoc on the church prior to his conversion on the road to Damascus.

According to Josephus, Theophilus was relieved of his high priestly duties when Agrippa I passed his office over to Simon, son of Boethus. From the writings of Luke, we learn that even after he was deposed Theophilus was still held in high esteem by many, including Luke.[99]

From here, Luke moves to the beautiful story of Zacharias and Elisabeth and God's promise to give them a son who would be the forerunner of Messiah. Following this, the angel Gabriel appears to a young virgin girl called Mary, living in Nazareth and probably still a teenager, and informs her that she will have a son called Jesus, the Son of the Most High.[100]

The two related and pregnant women then get together to share their joy. In Luke 1:46–55, we have what has become known as Mary's Magnificat, which comes from the first word in the Latin translation, which means "magnifies." This beautiful song is the first of three hymns in Luke 1–2 and is filled with Old Testament scriptures. It reveals the heart of a young girl which has been saturated with the Word of God. Drawn from numerous allusions to the Law, the psalms, and the prophets, the utterance is a virtual recitation of the Old Testament covenant promises of God. Following her three-month visit to the home of Elisabeth, Mary then returns to her home.[101]

Following the birth of John the Baptist and his subsequent circumcision, the voice of Zacharias is restored:

> Zacharias was only supposed to offer incense then come out to pronounce the familiar blessing of num. 6; 23–27 on the people who were waiting on the Temple Court… This passage

---

[99] William Whiston, ed., *The Works of Josephus* (Peabody, MA: Hendrickson Publishers, 1987), 410.

[100] *Liberty Bible Commentary*, 2008–2009.

[101] MacArthur, *The MacArthur Study Bible*, 1512. See notation Luke 1:46–55.

> is known as the Benedictus (the first word of Vs 68 in the Latin translation… it is liberally sprinkled with OT "and illusions). When Zacharias was struck mute in the Temple (v. 20), he was supposed to deliver the benediction… So it is fitting that when his speech was restored, the first words out of his mouth were this inspired benediction.[102]

Luke 2 encompasses the birth of Christ in Bethlehem and is probably one of the most familiar passages in all of Scripture, as it is read many hundreds of times around the world every Christmas (Luke 2:1–20). There's nothing more beautiful than a well-rehearsed Christmas pageant featuring Mary and Joseph doting over their very special baby. The shepherds are there as well as the wise men (always three) from Persia. The manger scene, complete with animals, real, pictured or imagined, reminds us again that Mary and Joseph found themselves in this very humble dwelling after being denied accommodations in an overcrowded motel. We are also left with the strong assumption that Mary was already experiencing labour pains when they arrived at the stable, giving birth to the baby Jesus almost immediately.

This all makes for a very touching scene, but one that is somewhat distanced from the account in the Bible. Luke 2:6 doesn't express the sense of urgency we imagine, instead depicting the birth of Jesus taking place a number of days later.

The wise men were probably still in Persia, their now-famous journey yet to come over the next two years. Their number is unknown, but their three gifts is probably the detail that causes us to think there were three. Tradition has even named them, but history leaves them anonymous. Historians differ as to whether they were Gentiles who represented a religious caste from their native Persia, or Jews descended from the Jewish dispersion of 586 BC when the Babylonians under Nebuchadnezzar destroyed Jerusalem and took many of the Israelites into captivity.

---

[102] Ibid., 1511–1533. See notation Luke 1:21, 1:68–79.

According to Matthew 2, they visited the Lord Jesus in his home where they presented Him with their gifts of gold, frankincense, and myrrh. What is most remarkable about their visit is that they fell down before Jesus and worshipped him. This tells us something of the status of Jesus, for only God is to be worshipped (Matthew 2:11, 4:10).

We now know that many of the homes in Palestine two thousand years ago were multi-storied and built into a hillside. Incorporated into the upper floor or nestled into the downstairs living area was a guest room which in Luke 2:7 is called a *kataluma*, (from the Greek). The King James Version translates this as an inn, which brings to mind a motel or lodging house, but that doesn't properly represent the meaning of *kataluma*.

Joseph had relatives in Bethlehem, his hometown, and we can be sure that he sought lodging with them. With the guest room filled to capacity, they were then offered accommodations on the lower floor, which was often used as a shelter for domestic animals and usually fitted with a feeding trough, or manger, carved into the floor or built into a wall. This provided a place of safety for animals at night.

We often project biblical terminology onto our culture, thus giving a very distorted picture. There is often an innkeeper in our Christmas plays, a character who is often maligned for denying accommodations to Joseph and his pregnant wife. In the Bible, there is no innkeeper and no inn. This takes nothing away from what transpired, but we now have a more realistic picture of those long-ago events. There is no doubt that the arrival of the baby Jesus aroused great excitement, with many friends, relatives, and shepherds crowding into the home to see this beautiful baby boy.[103]

As Christ is brought to the temple to be presented by His parents, they encounter a man called Simeon who, filled with the Holy Spirit, gives the wonderful words that are known as Nunc Dimittis[104] in Luke

---

[103] *Uncovering the Real Nativity* (Petersburg, KY: Answers in Genesis, 2012), 8–10.

[104] This term refers to the first words in Latin of Simeon's song of praise. It means "You can now dismiss."

2:29–35.[105] These Latin words express a prayer to God (Luke 2:29–32) as well as Simeon's prophetic warning to Mary and Joseph (Luke 2:34–35). Simeon sees salvation in the person of Christ (Luke 2:30) and then warns His parents that Christ will bring division and opposition. This amazing prophecy of Simeon tells of salvation for both Jews and Gentiles (Luke 2:32). His words reveal the appalling truth about the depth of Jewish apostasy.

When Simeon lifted little Jesus into his arms, he realized that God had kept His promise, allowing him to see the Messiah before his passing. This spirit-filled individual is found nowhere else in the Bible. There is another powerful prophecy in Luke 2:35, where Simeon tells Mary that she will feel the sword pierce her own soul at the crucifixion of her Son.[106]

Following Simeon's prophecy, we meet the aged Anna, who lived in the temple precinct. She fasted and prayed constantly, offering a prayer of thanks for redemption in Israel.

By the time we find our way to the later verses of this chapter, we find the twelve-year-old Christ in the temple speaking with teachers who were amazed at His knowledge and understanding.

Luke 3:1–22 deals with the ministry of John the Baptist, which is followed by Luke's genealogy (Luke 3:23–38). The temptation of Christ is then given in vivid detail in Luke 3, and following it we become acquainted with the public ministry of Christ.

Some of the first disciples are brought into Christ's inner circle in Luke 5. In the next chapter, Christ's following is solidified as He brings together His twelve disciples. A centurion's servant is healed in the early verses of Luke 7, which directly follows Christ's exposition of the Beatitudes in the latter part of Luke 6.

Some have wondered how Christ supported Himself after leaving home and entering into an itinerant ministry. At least part of the answer is found in Luke 8:1–3, where a group of women are recognized as patron supporters of Christ and His disciples. One of these women

---

[105] Brand, ed., *The Holman Illustrated Bible Dictionary*, 1171.

[106] MacArthur, *The MacArthur Study Bible*, 1515–1516. See notations 225 and 235.

is Mary Magdalene, who probably came from the Galilean town of Magdala. This faithful follower of the Lord Jesus was delivered from disease and demon possession, but there's not one shred of evidence to show she was a prostitute, as is falsely assumed by some.

Two other women named are Joanna and Susanna. Joanna, who's also mentioned in Luke 24:10, was a part of Herod's household and possibly supplied valuable information to Luke about the royal quarter which he incorporated into his Gospel. Susanna is mentioned nowhere else and was probably well known to Luke. There is the mention of "many others" who aren't named.[107]

Later in Luke 8, Jesus stills the sea and continues His healing ministry. The twelve disciples are then very active in Luke 9, and here we read of the transfiguration and the test of real greatness. The seventy are sent out in the following chapter and Jesus tells the story of the Good Samaritan. Instructions about prayer introduce Luke 11 and the Pharisees receive a blistering rebuke from Christ. The latter part of Luke 12 speaks of the division that the presence of Christ brings. From Luke 13:22–35, we see Christ teaching in the villages while in the next chapter we are introduced to the parables of the guests and the dinner.

## A SHOCKING FINALE

In Luke 15, we find one of the most gripping stories ever told when Jesus gives a moving account of a man and his two sons. One writer has commented that "it is hands down, the greatest five minutes of storytelling ever."[108]

This is actually the last of a trilogy of parables, being preceded by the parables of the lost sheep and the lost coin. The parable of the unrighteous steward is found in Luke 16.

---

[107] Ibid., 1528. See notation 8:2.

[108] John MacArthur, *A Tale of Two Sons: The Inside Story of a Father, His Sons, and a Shocking Murder* (Nashville, TN: Thomas Nelson, 2008), 18.

The key to these four parables is found in Luke 15:1–2 and 16:14. The rising animosity of the scribes and Pharisees against the Lord Jesus was fuelled by His willingness to embrace the tax gatherers, prostitutes, and other undesirables who in their opinion were unworthy of the grace of God. The timeframe here is significant, as Christ was only months away from His death by crucifixion; the religious establishment already had the wheels rolling to bring about His destruction.

The perceptive Pharisees knew that the son who stayed behind and refused to receive his wayward brother, even venting rage against his father for showing mercy to the prodigal son, was clearly a picture of them while Christ was represented by the loving father.

While many readers identify closely with the prodigal son based on their own experience, the context and historical setting strongly suggest that the real focus of the story should rest on the older son.

This, the longest of Jesus's parables, ends abruptly in Luke 15:32 on the heels of a heated verbal exchange between the father and his older son, who in a demeaning manner had referred to his younger sibling as *"this son of yours"* (Luke 15:30, ESV). He defiantly refused to accept his father's unconditional offer of love and forgiveness to his remorseful and repentant son, who after years of recklessness and rebellion had returned to his father's welcoming embrace. The son who had remained at home would grant no mercy to his younger brother, who upon his return had openly acknowledged the awfulness of his sin as he ran into the welcoming arms of his loving father (Luke 15:18–21).

We are left to wonder what happens, but in this setting there can be only one ending. The Pharisees, represented by the older son—the religious elite, clothed in their robes of self-righteousness—resented and resisted the granting of God's favour to sinners, represented by the younger son—the very lowest in society, coming in their sinful rags to receive love and forgiveness from the Lord Jesus, represented by the father.

We long for a happy ending, but instead there is a tragic ending that cannot be avoided. These words from John MacArthur tell of a stunning conclusion:

> We therefore know how the tale really ended, then, don't we? It is not a happy ending. Instead, it's another shocking plot turn. In fact, it is the greatest shock and outrage of all time. They killed Him. Since the father figure in the parable represents Christ and the elder brother is a symbol of Israel's religious elite, in effect, the true ending to the story, as written by the scribes and Pharisees themselves, ought to read something like this; the elder son was outraged at his father. He picked up a piece of lumber and beat him to death in front of everyone. I told you it was a shocking ending.[109]

What must not be lost sight of here is that almost immediately the Lord Jesus gives another parable, but notice how in Luke 16:1, which begins the story of the unrighteous steward, He turns away from the Pharisees and addresses the disciples about the impossibility of serving both God and money. Apparently the Pharisees hung around, though, and in Luke 16:14 they chided and ridiculed the Lord Jesus.

Only a few months later, they wrote their own ending to the parable of the prodigal son: "Securing the grudging cooperation of the Roman authorities and even the collusion of Herod—they had Him crucified."[110] With the Lord's stinging words of rebuke still ringing in their ears, they planned, plotted, and participated in the murder of their Messiah.

---

[109] Ibid., 194–195.

[110] Ibid., 197.

The story does have a happy ending after all, because on the third day the Lord Jesus rose from the dead in resurrection power, thus securing our free and full redemption.

## TWO MEN, TWO DESTINIES

Luke 16:19–31 tells the story of the rich man and Lazarus. The rich man finds himself in horrible torment following his death while the poor man is comforted in Abraham's bosom. The lesson is clear for all to see: there is an eternal destiny for every human being which entails either an eternity shut away from the presence of a holy God or an eternity of peace and joy in His blessed presence.

The next chapter tells of the cleansing of ten lepers with only one, a Samaritan, returning to give thanks to the Great Physician (Luke 17:16).

The second coming occupies the latter part of Luke 17, and in the next chapter comes the story of the rich young ruler who, trapped by his riches, refuses to give his heart to Christ. In Luke 19, the small-of-stature Zacchaeus is blessed by having the Lord Jesus as a guest in his home as well as his heart. The triumphal entry comes later in the chapter. The issue of one's tribute to Caesar, as well as the resurrection, form a large part of Luke 20. The following chapter has to do largely with future events, including the coming of Christ.

Luke 22 covers many topics as we are rushed along to the reason Christ came: the crucifixion. Those topics include the Passover, the Lord's Supper, true greatness, the betrayal, Gethsemane, the arrest, and Jesus's appearance before the Sanhedrin. In the next passage, Jesus comes before Pilate, and then Herod, after which we read of Pilate's futile attempt to set Jesus free. This is then followed by the crucifixion and the burial of Christ.

The final chapter provides a riveting account of the resurrection and a replay of some of the lively conversation that took place on the

Emmaus Road. I've always felt a sense of warmth and excitement as I read Luke 24:32 in the King James Version, which is hard to improve upon: *"And they said one to another, Did not our heart burn within us, while he talked with us by the way, and while he opened to us the scriptures?"* (KJV)

This comment from the *New Bible Commentary* is worth noting.

> This narrative could be taken to imply that the resurrection and ascension both happened on the same day, Easter Sunday. But this would contradict Luke's further account in Acts 1. It follows that what is here described briefly and compactly has taken place over a longer period of time.[111]

Luke ends his Gospel with the ascension and begins his second book with the same event in Acts 1:9–11.

The closing verses of Luke's Gospel tell of praising and blessing God in the temple. Does it not seem appropriate that the centre of worship in the Old Testament became the first meeting place for the New Testament church? There were many rooms around the porticoes of the outer court which would have been available and suitable for these times of praise and worship.

---

[111] *The New Bible Commentary*, 1020.

# The Gospel According to John

**As with the other Gospels, this book is named after its author. Since John** was a very common name in early times, and since the author doesn't use his name in the writing, there has been some limited debate as to his identity. Against all arguments to the contrary, church tradition from the earliest times has identified the author as John the Apostle, a son of Zebedee (Matthew 10:2–4), who along with his brother James is referred to by Christ as one of the *"Sons of Thunder"* (Mark 3:17, ESV)

The evidence for John's identity is compelling. Irenaeus (AD 130–200), one of the early church fathers, was disciplined by Polycarp (AD 70–160), who was himself mentored by the Apostle John. Based on the testimony of Polycarp, the writings of Irenaeus testify that John the Apostle wrote his Gospel while living in Ephesus and at an advanced age.[112]

As we will see later, John is also credited with the authorship of 1–3 John, along with the book of Revelation. The Gospel record testifies that John and his brother James, together with Peter, were the three most intimate associates of Christ (Matthew 17:1, 26:37). There is a

112 *The New Bible Commentary*, 1021.

strong tradition that John left Jerusalem before its destruction in AD 70, escaped to Ephesus, and was subsequently exiled to Patmos, where he wrote the Revelation.[113]

John's name means "Yahweh (Jehovah) is gracious."

There are twenty-one chapters in John's Gospel broken into:

- The Prologue (1:1–18)
- I Am the Voice (1:19–34)
- The Lamb of God (1:35–51)
- Water Turned to Wine (2:1–12)
- The House of Prayer (2:13–25)
- You Must Be Born Again (3:1–36)
- Jesus in Galilee and the Woman of Samaria (4:1–54)
- Healing at Bethesda (5:1–17)
- The Resurrection (5:18–32)
- Four Witnesses (5:33–47)
- The Miracle on Golan Heights (6:1–14)
- Jesus Walks on the Water (6:15–25)
- The Words of Christ (6:26–71)
- Jesus at the Feast (7:1–53)
- Neither Do I Condemn You (8:1–11)
- The Light of the World (8:12–30)
- The Truth Shall Set You Free (8:31–59)
- The Man Born Blind Is Healed (9:1–41)
- The Good Shepherd (10:1–21)
- The Deity of Christ (10:22–42)
- The Raising of Lazarus (11:1–57)
- Jesus Enters Jerusalem, Foretells His Death (12:1–50)
- The Lord's Supper and the Betrayal (13:1–38)
- Let Not Your Heart Be Troubled (14:1–31)
- Jesus Is the Vine (15:1–27)
- The Holy Spirit, Prayer (16:1–33)

[113] MacArthur, *The MacArthur Study Bible*, 1569.

- The High Priestly Prayer (17:1–26)
- Betrayal and Denial (18:1–40)
- The Crucifixion (19:1–42)
- He Is Risen (20:1–31)
- Do You Love Me? (21:1–25)

## SUMMARY

Though he is never mentioned by name, the evidence is overwhelming that John the Apostle is the author of the Gospel that bears his name. From the earliest days of the church, John has usually been identified with the unnamed person in John 13:23, 19:26, 20:2, and 21:7, 20 who is referred to as the one whom Jesus loved. When one considers the important part John plays in the ministry of Christ, it is remarkable that he chooses not to state his own name in his Gospel, which obviously reveals the humility and modesty that were an integral part of his character.

The Gospel of John was written by the author at an advanced age, possibly fifty years after the resurrection. According to the early church fathers, John was fully aware of the other Gospels but decided to write his own unique version of the ministry of Christ, which is referred to by Clement of Alexandria (AD 150–215) as a "spiritual Gospel."[114]

More than any other Gospel writer, John gives us a more complete picture of who Jesus is and what He came to do. His writing is one of certainty, using the word *believe* more than one hundred times. He is the only Gospel writer to give us a precise statement as to the purpose of his dissertation, which is enunciated in John 20:30–31:

> *And truly Jesus did many other signs in the presence of His disciples, which are not written in this book; but these are written that you may believe that Jesus is the Christ, the Son of God, and that believing you may have life in His name.* (NKJV)

---

[114] *ESV Study Bible*, 2015.

No less than eight times, John writes emphatic "I am" statements that identify the Lord Jesus as our God and Messiah. He also provides us with a record of eight miracles performed by Christ that further enforce His claim to deity, with six of them given only in John's Gospel. Even Mark's short Gospel, which contains nineteen miracles, makes no mention of these six supernatural events.

Many of the major themes that appear in John are introduced in the prologue (John 1:1–18), and more particularly the major theme that Jesus is the Christ, the Son of God (John 1:12, 14, 18).

The opening words of John's Gospel are a throwback to the opening phrase of Genesis, which referenced the beginning of the time-space-material universe. The verb "was" points to the eternal pre-existence of the Lord Jesus Christ, who is indeed the eternal God, the second Person of the Trinity.

There is no genealogy in John's Gospel because Christ, being God, has none, as He has always been. John is the only writer of Scripture to employ the term "Word" (*Logos*) in reference to Christ. The word *logos* carries the idea of divine self-expression, or speech, and has a rich Old Testament heritage in which we see the effectiveness of God's Word. Things come into being as God speaks, and as He speaks He relates personally to His people (Genesis 1:3, 9; 15:1; Psalm 33:6; 107:20; Isaiah 55:10–11).

John has borrowed the Greek word *logos* from the writings of Greek philosophers in which its impersonal usage signified the principle of divine reason, mind, and wisdom. Drawing from the Old Testament vocabulary, John gives the *Logos* (Word) a divine personality and theologically presents Christ as the Word who is the source of all intelligence, wisdom, and power. The term is used as a bridge between Jews and Gentiles where the usage of *logos* was familiar to both.[115]

It is with this powerful and attention-getting statement that John enters into his Gospel, emphatically stating his case that Christ was fully man yet without sin (Hebrews 4:15).

---

[115] F.F. Bruce, *The Gospel & Epistles of John* (Grand Rapids, MI: William B. Eerdmans, 1983), 28–31.

Only in John's Gospel do we learn that the length of Jesus' public ministry was about 3½ years by counting the Passover feasts. John is saturated with symbolic representations from ordinary life. Jesus used common things (such as water, bread, light, a vine and its branches, a loving shepherd and his pet sheep) to teach spiritual truths. The Gospel of John was written not so much to tell the historical facts of Jesus' brief stay on earth but to ask the question: What does His coming mean?[116]

From his carefully worded introduction in which he firmly establishes the divinity of Jesus Christ, John takes us to the ministry of John the Baptist, the forerunner of the Lord Jesus. Unlike the other Gospel writers, the Apostle John never adds the appendage "the Baptist" to John's name but leaves us to assume that whenever he refers to John he means John the Baptist. Skipping details that are documented in other writings, John takes us to the ministry of Christ in John 1:35–51.

## A SPIRITED DEBATE

John 2 takes us to a wedding feast in Cana of Galilee where Jesus, His mother, and His disciples were present. Approached by His mother with the news that they are out of wine, Jesus asked that six stone waterpots, usually reserved for water used for ceremonial washings, be filled with water (John 2:6–7). When the ruler of the feast tasted the contents of the waterpots, it was no longer water but an excellent wine.

This is the first of eight signs, or miracles, recorded by John, aside from the resurrection, that strengthen his argument that Christ was the promised Messiah. By the time we get to the end of John 11, we will be conversant with seven of these signs.

[116] *New American Standard Bible, Key Word Study Bible*, 1396.

Before listing these eight miracles so we can spot them as we read John's Gospel, I will comment in more detail on the first miracle. The story of the water being turned into wine by the Lord Jesus, along with Paul's comment in 1 Timothy 5:23, has spurred endless debate about the place of alcoholic beverages in the life of the Christian. Much attention is usually focused on the nature of the wine in John 2:3–9. Was it just grape juice or was it a fermented beverage?

We do know that much of the wine in the New Testament era was intoxicating but was also diluted to such an extent that it would take enormous amounts to even come near to bringing someone to a state of inebriation. We also know that many of the wines were pure grape juice and were a valued source of refreshment and nutrition. We are aware from the study of ancient culture and the Scriptures that wine was often distinguished from strong drink, which was strictly prohibited from consumption.

For Christians who play fast and loose with their Christian testimony, the Scripture provides valid principles for all cultures and generations. Romans 14:21 is just one of many verses that warn us about the effects our actions have on others. As far back as Leviticus 10:9, the Levites were forbidden to drink wine or strong drink when they entered the tabernacle. Some Bible scholars are convinced that the judgment that befell the sons of Aaron, Nadab and Abihu, resulted from their entering into priestly service while in a drunken state. According to Proverbs 20:1, wine is a mocker and strong drink is raging, and both can leave the partaker in an intoxicated state. The entirety of Proverbs 23:20-35 is a clear and concise indictment against the use of intoxicating drinks and presents a strong case for abstinence.

We would feel rather uncomfortable in the presence of Billy Sunday, a one-time professional baseball player turned evangelist. In one blistering sermon after another, he preached against the debilitating effects of alcohol. He saw some of his best friends go to an early grave because of alcoholism and he often pointed out that their downward slide began with their first drink. Months before some of his evangelistic campaigns, scores of tavern owners and liquor establishments braced themselves for closure or bankruptcy, so powerful was the influence of Sunday's preaching. When Sunday's converts came down the sawdust trail, they left their thirst for liquor at the altar. Many had already slid into lives of debauchery and degradation, having lost their livelihood, marriages, families, and friendships to the effects of drunkenness and loose living.[117]

On the evening of April 14, 1865, President Abraham Lincoln and his wife entered Ford's theatre in Washington D.C. to enjoy a play while in a nearby saloon John Wilkes Booth was having a drink. Having bolstered himself with liquor, Booth left the saloon, went to the theatre, and shot the president. Only moments before Booth's arrival, the President's personal guard had exited the theatre to go down the street for a glass of beer. Think about it![118]

Born to Charles and Reine Chiniquy in 1809, Charles Chiniquy was raised in a Roman Catholic home and eventually became a Roman Catholic priest. Though it was uncommon for Roman Catholics of that era, Charles' mother was an avid Bible reader who often read the Scriptures with her young son.[119] Long before his conversion to Christ, before leaving the priesthood to enter the Protestant ministry, this Roman Catholic priest made significant changes to his lifestyle that would shame

---

[117] Lee Thomas, *The Billy Sunday Story* (Murfreesboro, TN: Sword of the Lord Publishers, 2005), 303–323.

[118] Perry E. Rockwood, *Booze: The Devil's Nuclear Bomb* (Halifax, NS: The Peoples Gospel Hour), 5.

[119] Charles Chiniquy, *Fifty Years in the Church of Rome* (Ontario, CA: Chick Publications, 1985), 13–15.

today's worldly minded Christians. Feeling that the smoking of tobacco was unworthy of his Christian calling, he abandoned his smoking habit. He became convicted about the coarseness of his speech and ceased to participate in off-colour jokes. He also stopped taking the Lord's name in vain and determined that his words would be a positive and uplifting influence to those to whom he ministered.[120]

Most significant was his change of attitude toward the consumption of liquor. After being exposed to the ravages of the liquor traffic in his parish, along with seeing alcoholic priests in a drunken state even as they performed the mass with their constituents, he determined to adopt the practice of temperance and encouraged others to do the same.[121] Thousands were delivered from the evil effects of alcohol as Chiniquy delivered his message of temperance to all who would listen.

As bars closed and his message spread, the most noticeable difference came in people's homes. Men no longer came home drunk to terrified wives and children who were often the innocent victims of drunken outrages. Children were no longer going to bed hungry because their parents had spent all their money on liquor. Women who were selling themselves on street corners in order to satisfy their insatiable appetite for alcohol became moral and respectable citizens and were enabled to become honourable wives to their husbands and proper mothers to their children.[122]

The so-called harmless social drink has opened the door to a host of social problems that are tearing our society apart. The drug addiction epidemic that has taken on global proportions can be traced to what is still our number one drug problem, the

---

[120] Ibid., 22–71.

[121] Charles Chiniquy, *Forty Years in the Church of Christ* (Toronto, CA: Wittenberg Publications, 1987), 30–33.

[122] Chiniquy, *Fifty Years in the Church of Rome*, 118, 144–151, 174–176,

unbridled consumption of alcohol, along with all its attendant evils.

My determination to never allow alcohol to pass my lips gives me the assurance that I will never become addicted to its deadly influence or suffer from its many debilitating consequences. My choice never to offer alcohol to my neighbour means I will never be held responsible should they ever succumb to its deceptive and destructive effects (Habakkuk 2:15).

While taking a strong position against liquor in my personal life and its use in general, it is not for me to stand in judgment of others. I remain unconvinced that the Scriptures teach total abstinence from all intoxicating drinks, but abuse of such is clearly addressed and condemned. The key element in any discussion is that of moderation along with freedom of choice (1 Timothy 3:8, 1 Peter 4:3–4).

Paul's admonition to his young understudy in 1 Timothy 5:23 weighs strongly in favour of a fermented drink rather than ordinary grape juice for which such advisement would not be necessary. The context of Matthew 11:18–19 seems also to warrant a reference to fermented wine, but not necessarily; the Greek word for wine here could just as easily have referred to sweet juice of the vine. Our Lord Jesus wasn't condemned for eating but for an overindulgence of food of which He was innocent. He is not judged for drinking wine in moderation but is falsely accused of drinking to excess.

These thoughts come from J. Stephen Lang:

> The Bible definitely does *not* prohibit drinking alcohol. The only people who abstained were the Nazirites, and they were only a small group within Israel. Drunkenness and the danger it brings are condemned, and Proverbs 20:1 summarizes the biblical view of drunkenness: "Wine is a mocker, strong drink is a brawler, and

> whoever is led astray by it is not wise." In other words, don't let drinking turn you into a fool. Proverbs 31:6 reads, "Give strong drink to him who is perishing, and wine to those who are bitter of heart"—a recognition that in the days before pain relievers and anesthetics, alcohol could serve a useful purpose. Jesus' miracle of turning water into wine suggests that He did not disapprove of drinking it (John 2).
>
> The American Temperance Movement arose in the 1870s, and many Christians were at the front of that movement. In time, there was a shift from temperance (which only means moderation) to tee-totaling and prohibition. The result was National Prohibition from 1919–1932 [in the U.S.]- a social experiment that failed.[123]

*The New Bible Dictionary* gives us this valid and balanced assessment of wine and strong drink in both Testaments of the Scriptures:

> Among a considerable number of synonyms used in the OT the most common are *yayin* (usually translated wine) "and sekar (usually translated strong drink)." These terms are frequently used together and they are employed irrespective of whether the writer is commending wine and strong drink as desirable or warning against its dangers. A third word, tiros, sometimes translated "new" or "sweet wine", has often been regarded as unfermented and therefore unintoxicating wine... [but] it is capable of being used in a bad sense equally with the others... Naturally in a land and climate particularly suited to

[123] J. Stephen Lang, *1001 Things You Always Wanted to Know About the Bible But Never Thought to Ask* (Nashville, TN: Nelson Books, 1999), 119.

the cultivation of the vine, we find that wine was often associated with grain and together they stand for a full and adequate supply of food and of the good gifts of life. They can be promised therefore as the tokens of the blessings of God (Gn. 27:28)… as a discipline, however, they are on occasion to be dispensed with as when a man engages in priestly service (Lv. 10:9), or in the case of a Nazirite during the course of his vow (Nu. 6:3)… Evidence is by no means lacking, however, that even to those who accepted the agricultural way of life the dangers of strong drink were apparent. The warnings of the Book of Proverbs are clear and in the time of Isaiah even the priests fell into the snare… These two aspects of wine, its use and its abuse, its benefits and its curse, its acceptance in Gods sight and its abhorrence, are interwoven into the OT so that it may gladden the heart of man (Ps. 104:15) or cause his mind to err (Is. 28:7) it can be associated with merriment (Ec. 10:19) or with anger (Is. 5:11) it can be used to uncover the shame of Noah (Gn. 9:21) or in the hands of Melchizedek to honor Abraham (Gn. 14:18)… Wine may represent that which God himself has prepared (Pr. 9:5)… on the other hand it may equally well represent the intoxicating influence of Babylonian supremacy which brings ruin (Je. 51:7)…

In the NT the common word is Gk. onios (cf. Heb. Yayin)… The references in the NT are very much fewer in number, but once more the good and the bad aspects are equally apparent... John the Baptist is to abstain from wine… but this does not imply that of itself that wine is evil, for Jesus is not only present at the wedding in Cana of Galilea, but when the wine fails he replenishes the supply in extraordinarily ample measure... Methaphorically in the NT the word "wine" is again used in both a good and bad sense. The latter is found several times in Revelation, where the inhabitants of the earth are depicted as having been made drunk by the fornication of Babylon (Rev. 7:2) while she herself is drunk with their blood (Rev. 17:6)... Certainly on the day of Pentecost there were many who took the evidence of the spirit to be nothing else than the result of strong drink. This same interpretation had been placed long before upon the movement of the lips of Hannah as she prayed in the presence of Eli, a supposed fault which Eli was quicker to rebuke in her than in his own sons (1 Sa. 1:14)... Timothy is exhorted by Paul to take a little wine because of its medicinal properties (1 Tim. 5:23 cf. its application in a different form in the story of the Good Samaritan), but in the pastoral epistles there is a recognition of the grave dangers of excess... (1 Tim. 3:8; Tit. 2:3). This abuse is particularly unfitting within the church, for it is true that drunkenness is in general a sign of heedlessness in spiritual matters and a disregard of the imminent return of Christ (Rom. 13:13), how much more as it is to be deplored at the Lords table where it reveals not only a spirit of complete indifference towards God but a spirit of utter thoughtlessness in regard to those who stand together within the church fellowship (1 Cor. 11:21)... it may be said that while wine is not condemned as being without usefulness, it brings in the hands of sinful men such dangers of becoming uncontrolled that even those who count themselves to be strong would be wise to abstain, if not for their own sake, yet for the sake of weaker brethren. Romans 14:21[124]

[124] *The New Bible Dictionary*, 1242–1243.

So many valuable lessons are to be learned from John 2:1–11, the passage where Jesus turns water into wine in Cana. According to John 2:11, the disciples had become fully convinced as to who Christ was, having observed this astounding miracle.

Much of our discussion is taken up with what kind of wine was at issue, and whether it was fermented, and thus we lose sight of the great spiritual truths to be found here. In light of the custom and culture of the time, some are persuaded that the wine here was fermented. Others are convinced that this was newly minted wine fresh from the vine. The safest and most sensible stance is that we don't know and it doesn't matter.

The Apologetics Study Bible gives this response to John 2:6–7:

> Creating this much wine would seem to encourage drunkenness. Worse, this miracle seems to be frivolous from start to finish, hardly meeting any acute human need. On the other hand, wedding festivities often lasted for a week and an entire village could have been involved, so the amounts consumed by any individual at one time may have been quite moderate. Furthermore, one of the points of the miracle was to stress the new joy associated with Jesus' ministry and the kingdom He was inaugurating.[125]

Canadian Christians must resist the temptation to read this passage of Scripture through the filter of our modern culture. The wine here is not mixed with other ingredients in order to increase its potency. The drinking here is not geared to give the participants a buzz nor to lure them into binge drinking. These were religious Jews who were well-schooled in Old

[125] *The Apologetics Study Bible*, 1573–1574.

Testament law and well-versed in God's instruction concerning drunkenness and debauchery.

The celebrants were not only blessed with the presence of the Lord Jesus but were witness to His first miracle, which became the launching pad for His earthly ministry. Picture in your mind's eye what the scene must have looked like as Jesus filled the waterpots to the brim with new wine. One can almost feel the sheer joy that engulfed the gathering in Cana, with high-fives all around, lively music, dancing feet, and squeals of delight.

The wedding at Cana aptly pictured the Jewish nation two thousand years ago, which was only a shell of its former self. The words uttered by Mary in John 2:3, *"They have no wine"* (John 2:3, NKJV), speaks volumes of a people who had been left lifeless and empty by the endless round of rites, ritual, and ceremony. The promised Messiah was in their midst and he would not only fill their empty containers but soon fill their lives with His peace, joy, and life abundant. The ESV Study Bible notes, "The wedding party's running out of wine may be seen as symbolizing the spiritual barrenness of first-century Judaism, especially against an Old Testament background that viewed wine (but never drunkenness) as a sign of joy and God's blessing."[126]

Whatever the consistency of the wine, we know it was provided supernaturally by the Lord Jesus being witnessed by His mother Mary, the disciples, and all others who attended the wedding feast. The bride and groom would never forget their wedding day and would have so many fond memories to share with their children and grandchildren.

The following quote from *The Holman Illustrated Bible Dictionary* gives us an appreciation for the culture of Palestine in the first century of our era: "In NT times wine was kept

---

[126] *ESV Study Bible*, 2022. See Psalm 104:15, Proverbs 3:10, and Matthew 26:29.

in skin flasks and often diluted with water. It was also used as a medicine and disinfectant. Scripture condemns drunkenness and overindulgence but pictured wine as a part of the typical ancient meal."[127]

The discussion continues in this separate article, "New or Sweet Wine":

> New or sweet wine was likely wine from the first drippings of juice before the grapes had been trodden. Some interpreters argue that new wine was unfermented. Some texts in which it is mentioned, however, allude to its intoxicating effects Hosea 4:11; Acts 2:13. In the hot climate before the invention of refrigeration, it was not possible to keep wine many months past the harvest before fermentation began. Wine was considered a luxury item which could both gladden the heart (Psalm 105:15) or cloud the mind Isaiah 28:7; Hosea 4:11.[128]

Here is another summation of wine and intoxicating drinks:

> One characteristic of Hebrew poetry is the repetition of similar thoughts in couplets, such as the repeated objects "wine" and "intoxicating drink" in Prov. 31:4. These two items appear in parallel demonstrating that the author considered them in more or less the same light. In other passages, wine and intoxicating drink are similarly mentioned together (Lev. 10:9; 1 Samuel 1:15).
>
> There is evidence from later times that the difference between "wine" and "intoxicating drink" was one of concentration rather than formula. The juice of the

[127] Brand, ed., *The Holman Illustrated Bible Dictionary*, 1675.

[128] Ibid., 443.

> grapes was stored in full strength in jars soon after the squeezing process. When it came time to drink the juice, water was mixed with it. The amount of water added determined whether the product was considered "wine" or "intoxicating drink". In New Testament times we know that the most common mixture for "wine" was three or more parts of water for each portion of juice. "Intoxicating drink" was a mixture of juice and water with a stronger portion of juice. Drinking the juice without diluting it was thought to make one mad. So it was that Hannah's protested actions were due to grief, not to drunkenness because she had not been drinking an "intoxicating drink" or even wine (1 Samuel 1:15,16). Similarly, kings and princes were warned to abstain from anything that would obscure their reason causing them to fail in their responsibilities of leadership (Prov. 31:4,5).[129]

The world would be a much better place if there was no such thing as liquor, but the Bible doesn't condemn drinking in moderation. This is an area of personal choice and I would caution the reader to show due respect toward others of varied persuasions. As Romans 14:5 advises us, *"Let every man be fully persuaded in his own mind"* (KJV).

A well-researched and informative publication concerning the wines of the Bible was written by William Patton. He argues that many of the wines in the Bible were not fermented, including the wine of John 2. He presents a strong case for Christians not to drink intoxicating drinks of any kind. Not all will agree with his conclusions, but it is well-documented.

One of the more interesting notations is this quote taken from the works of Albert Barnes: "The wine of Judea was the

[129] *The Chronological Study Bible* (Nashville, TN: Thomas Nelson, 2008), 900.

pure juice of the grape, without any mixture of alcohol, and commonly weak and harmless. It was the common drink of the people, and did not tend to produce intoxication."[130]

Patton also quotes Dr. Herrick Johnson extensively. Here is Johnson's assessment as to whether drinking intoxicating beverages by a Christian cannot be termed a sin:

> I do not believe that the drinking of wine is a sin per say. I do not believe that a church court should make it a matter of discipline. But I do believe that the Christian is known by precept or example to be an advocate of the use of the cup, takes upon himself a fearful responsibility. Effect of such precept or example is felt far beyond the circle of those with whom such Christian comes in contact. The higher the position of the man [or woman], the wider will be the influence of his [or her] word or deed. And among the tens of thousands who were nearly swept to ruin by alcohol, there may be those to whom his [or her] shining example has been a stumbling block and an occasion to fall.[131]

A far different view is taken by Albert Garner, evidenced by his view of social drinking: "There can be no social drinking of intoxicating beverages without breaking one's church covenant and the Word of God. It is a sin for any child of God to partake of strong drink except a medical prescription."[132]

Over the years, I have struggled with this issue. Should a local church mandate that its members abstain from all

---

[130] William Patton, *Bible Wine or the Laws of Fermentation* (Little Rock, AR: Challenge Press), 105.

[131] Ibid., 109.

[132] Albert Garner, *The Church Covenant: My Sacred Vows* (Texarkana, TX: Bogard Press, 2000), 46.

alcoholic beverage? I am now persuaded that the church, or a pastor, may advise in accordance with the principles of the Bible, but forcing the issue of teetotaling on church members goes beyond the bounds of Scripture.

For all who are jealous for the Word of God, the Word of God gives sane and sensible counsel. The use of alcoholic beverages is a sensitive matter in the Christian circles, but we are cautioned not to impose our personal convictions on others. We must be careful not to go beyond the Scriptures, but allow for individual choice.

The following quote presents a reasonable balance in its approach to the turning water into wine in John 2:

> There are some Christians who claim that Jesus would never create anything alcoholic and that the "wine" Jesus makes in this story must be unfermented grape juice. The theory is fascinating, but biblically unsupportable. The same Greek word for wine in this passage (oinos) is used elsewhere in the Bible to refer to a liquid that has the ability to purify a wound (Luke 10:34) or cause drunkenness (Eph. 5:18) or even addiction (Titus 2:3). These are qualities of alcohol, not vitamin C. In the Septuagint (the Greek translation of the Hebrew Bible that was read and quoted by the New Testament authors, *oinos* most often translates *yayin* which is the Hebrew word for fermented wine (as opposed to *tirosh* or *mishreh*, usually meaning unfermented juice or juice that is not fully fermented). Also See Luke 7:33–34 where, unlike John the Baptist, Jesus garners the reputation among the religious conservatives of his day of being a "drunkard" because he drinks *oinois*. The Bible (Old Testament and New Testament) often warns against

> the potential negative effects of alcohol and teaches against drunkenness, but does not mandate complete abstinence. That is a choice left to every individual… (2 Timothy 2:14, 23; 1 Timothy 6:4)[133]

For me, the decision is an easy one. Many of the mounting social problems in our society are a direct result of the consumption of alcohol. For believers, the issue becomes even more pronounced; the so-called harmless social drink does nothing to enhance our testimony for Christ and may even dampen our witness to a watching world or other Christians. This practice most certainly falls into the category of the questionable.

Then, too, there are those who are recovering alcoholics who need not be tempted to return to an addiction that in many cases has very nearly destroyed them. Churches have every good reason not to include fermented wine in the communion service. I will submit without hesitation that there is not one redeeming virtue in liquor and God's people would be benefited to live without it… and so would our society.

> *For if your brother is grieved by what you eat, you are no longer walking in love. By what you eat, do not destroy the one for whom Christ died. So do not let what you regard as good be spoken of as evil.* (Romans 14:15–16, ESV)

A later verse in this same chapter gives sane and sensible counsel for all who are jealous for the glory of God and the advancement of his kingdom: *"It is good not to eat meat or drink wine or do anything that causes your brother to stumble"* (Romans 14:21, ESV).

---

[133] Bruxy Cavey, *The End of Religion: Encountering the Subversive Spirituality of Jesus* (Colorado Springs, CO: NavPress, 2007), 245.

In the context of Romans 14, the wine referenced in John 2 is surely not grape juice or a citrus drink but a fermented beverage that is potentially harmful and inebriating.

## MESSIAH AND MIRACLES

John has given us eight signs (miracles) that identify Christ as the promised Messiah.

1. Water Turned into Wine (John 2:1–11)
2. Healing of the Nobleman's Son (John 4:46–54)
3. Healing at the Pool of Bethesda (John 5:1–17)
4. Feeding of the Five Thousand (John 6:1–14)
5. Jesus Walks on the Water (John 6:15–25)
6. Healing of the Man Born Blind (John 9:1–41)
7. The Raising of Lazarus (John 11:1–46)
8. The Second Miraculous Catch of Fish (John 21:1–11)

The first miraculous catch of fish is recorded in Luke 5:1–11, yet some students of Scripture see another miracle in the last chapter of John when Jesus creates a breakfast of bread and fish and waits to feed the hungry fishermen. Some have questioned the validity of John 21:11, where the fish count is given as exactly 153. This verse proves that John was an eyewitness of these events. The fish were large and, as was customary, carefully counted before being hauled off to market.

In John 3, a Pharisee called Nicodemus seeks out the Lord Jesus under cover of darkness. The Greek wording here shows Nicodemus to be a well-respected rabbi and a teacher of the highest order. His failure to grasp the significance and meaning of the new birth experience was symbolic of the moral and spiritual bankruptcy of Jewish religion at the time of Christ. The instruction of Jesus was based solidly on the Old

Testament Scriptures, which should have been familiar to this educated religious leader (Ezekiel 36:24–27, Numbers 19:17–19, Psalm 51:9–10, Isaiah 32:15, 44:3–5, 55:1–3, Jeremiah 2:13, Joel 2:28–29).

Nicodemus is mentioned in two later chapters of John's Gospel (John 7:50, 19:39) and we have every reason to believe that this influential Jewish teacher embraced the Lord Jesus as his Messiah.

In John 4, Jesus positions Himself near to a piece of real estate that Jacob had deeded to his son Joseph in Genesis 33:18–20), demonstrating a geographical and personal attachment to Old Testament patriarchal history. This is also the spot where Joseph was buried (Joshua 24:32).

While Jesus rests near a well, an unsuspecting woman from a nearby Samaritan city arrives, and she is about to experience a face to face encounter with the Son of God. Despised by her Jewish neighbours and torn apart by a series of broken relationships, she comes late in the day, around 6:00 p.m., with the hope of drawing water unnoticed. Her life is changed forever when Jesus reveals Himself to her as the promised Messiah.

As the disciples come upon the scene, the woman leaves her waterpot and scurries home to share the good news that she has found the Messiah.

John 5 begins with the healing of the man at the pool of Bethesda. This pool was located near the north wall of the city of Jerusalem and is identified by many today with the dual pool complex that lies near the present-day Church of St. Anne. The ruins surrounding this pool strongly indicate the presence of five porches at some time in the distant past.[134] Some ancient accounts record the waters here being red with minerals, possibly indicated that they were fed by intermittent springs high in mineral content.

The word Bethesda is the Greek transliteration of a Hebrew or Aramaic name which means "house of mercy" or "house of outpouring."[135]

---

[134] Bruce, *The Gospel & Epistles of John*, 121–123.

[135] *ESV Study Bible*, 2040. See notation John 5:2.

The man who was healed wouldn't likely have been able to pull himself into the pool. He had been stricken with a debilitating disease for nearly four decades and his pitiful condition was well known in his home area. His marvellous healing was known almost immediately and the Jews rose up against Christ with a vengeance, especially when the Lord Jesus addressed God as his Father (John 5:17–18).

The latter part of John 5:3 and all of John 5:4 are absent in many of the earlier manuscripts, suggesting they were a later insertion by copyists.[136]

John presents us with no less than eight witnesses to the person and ministry of Christ, with half of them given in John 5. Before moving on to the next chapter, we will list these eight witnesses:

1. John the Baptist (John 5:33)
2. The Works of Christ (John 5:36)
3. The Father (John 5:37–38)
4. The Scriptures (John 5:39)
5. The Lord Jesus Himself (John 8:18)
6. Believers (John 14:12)
7. The Holy Spirit (John 15:26)
8. The Disciples (John 15:27)

John 6 tells us of how the Lord Jesus takes five loaves and two fish and multiplies them to provide enough food for as many as twenty thousand people. According to Matthew 14:21, there were five thousand men besides women and children.

Shortly thereafter, the Lord Jesus walks on the water to meet His disciples in their boat. This passage marks the beginning of the eight "I am" statements that are unique to John's Gospel. They are here given in the order in which they appear:

---

[136] *The New Bible Commentary*, 1036. This passage is discussed in greater detail in my book, *The Scripture in Translation.*

1. I am the bread of life. (John 6:35)
2. I am the light of the world. (John 8:12)
3. I am—an expression of His eternal existence and His deity. (John 8:24)[137]
4. I am the door of the sheep. (John 10:7)
5. I am the good shepherd. (John 10:11)
6. I am the resurrection and the life. (John 11:25)
7. I am the way, the truth, and the life. (John 14:6)
8. I am the vine. (John 15:5)

As Jesus teaches at the Feast of Booths, or Feast of Tabernacles, in John 7, there is division among His hearers concerning Him (John 7:12). On the last day of the feast, He speaks of the rivers of living water which refers to the ministry of the Holy Spirit (John 7:37–39).

The story of the woman caught in adultery is recorded in John 8. Because some of the early manuscripts don't record this account, some have questioned whether this was a later addition to the Scriptures. I am fully convinced there should be no question of its validity and that it belongs as part of the New Testament canon.

John 8:32 puts the Gospel in true perspective with a stern rebuke to all that is false: *"And you shall know the truth, and the truth shall make you free"* (NKJV).

The entirety of John 9 is occupied with the healing of the man who had been born blind. In the following chapter, Christ comes as the good Shepherd and speaks of the abundance of life He gives to His sheep (John 10:10–11).

The raising of Lazarus in John 11, which took place four days after the man's death, left no doubt in the minds of witnesses as to the true identity of the Lord Jesus. With a reminder from Martha that the body of her deceased brother was already in a state of decomposition, Jesus orders the stone removed from the entrance to the tomb (John 11:39) and then calls Lazarus to come out. As the gathering crowd gasps in

[137] Compare to Exodus 3:14.

breathless astonishment, Lazarus comes out of the grave in response to the voice of Christ.

The news of this miracle sends shockwaves to Jerusalem, with the Pharisees and chief priests plotting from this day forward to have Jesus put to death (John 11:53). So enraged are the Jewish religious leaders that they not only desire the death of Christ but also determine to put Lazarus to death as well (John 12:10). Here Lazarus had just been brought back from the dead and almost immediately he found himself in danger of being murdered by his own religious leaders.

Later in John 12, Jesus foretells His own death, even indicating the means by which it would be brought about (John 12:32–33). There are some scholars who feel that the Lazarus of this passage is to be identified with the Lazarus of Luke 16:20, but this fanciful theory has no evidence to support it. Lazarus was from a middle class family and lived with his two sisters, Mary and Martha, and had no need to beg at a rich man's table.

The Lord Jesus takes the place of a servant in John 13 as He washes the disciples' feet. This passage contains no command for us to do the same, but our attitude toward others ought to be one of humility and servanthood. Some Christian assemblies have tried to equate this with the ordinances of baptism and the Lord's table, but such a view has no scriptural support.

Following this event, Jesus predicts His own betrayal. The opening verses of John 14 are among the most familiar in all of the New Testament. These comforting verses are read at most Christian funeral services, but in context they are directed to His disciples who will soon witness His death, burial, resurrection, and ascension.

## GREATER WORKS?

In John 14:12, Jesus said, *"Most assuredly, I say to you, he who believes in Me, the works that I do he will do also; and greater works than these he will do, because I go to My Father"* (NKJV). This verse has been woefully twisted and made to mean something quite different from what our Saviour's really intended. This is especially true among ministries that seem to specialize in the spectacular and miraculous.

What did Jesus mean by these greater works? Does this mean that individual Christians have the same miracle-working powers as our Lord Jesus had when He walked among us? The short answer is an emphatic *no*, but I will explain myself more fully.

Have you met any Christians lately who can walk on water? Have you witnessed any believer in recent memory who was able to raise a four-days-in-the-grave man from the dead? Have you made the acquaintance of any follower of Jesus today who is able to take a small lunch and turn it into a grand feast for twenty thousand people?

This is not to suggest that the days of miracles are over, but even the disciples of Christ were limited in their powers and abilities. Raising the dead was witnessed in only a few isolated instances following the ascension of Christ. Not all sick people who came in contact with the apostles were healed. Paul was enabled to raise the young Eutychus from the dead in Acts 20:9–12, but he left Trophimus still sick at Miletus when he departed the city.

I've heard some believers quote this verse in a flippant manner and give the false impression that they can duplicate the miracles of Christ at will. Henry Krabbendam makes this thoughtful observation: "It is difficult to envision anyone able to produce miracles that are more numerous or impressive than those of Jesus. Surely, the miracles that accompanied His presence on earth are unsurpassed in quantity and quality."[138]

The context of John 14:12 is the clue to its meaning and understanding. Only a few verses later, Jesus speaks of the Holy Spirit who indwells every believer and enables us to experience His power as we witness to the unsaved around us. Jesus clearly meant greater works in *extent*, not in *power* as is erroneously implied by some (John 14:16–17). By the power of the indwelling of the Holy Spirit, Christians become

[138] Henry Krabbendam, "Scripture Twisting," *The Agony of Deceit* (Chicago, IL: Moody Bible Institute, 1990), 83.

witnesses to the whole world, bringing many to a saving knowledge of Christ. The emphasis here is not on physical miracles but rather on that which is spiritual, whereby many hundreds of thousands respond to the Gospel message and are swept into the kingdom of God.

These greater works find their connection in the ascension of Christ and the outpouring of the Holy Spirit, bringing the first two chapters of Acts into clear focus. Acts 1:8 is not only the book of Acts in capsule form but it is indicative of the church of Christ for more than two thousand years. It is estimated that more souls were saved in one day following the outpouring of the Holy Spirit in Acts than were brought by Christ in three years of ministry. This gigantic discipling ministry far outweighed anything that had ever gone before.

The ESV Study Bible further adds,

> These "greater works" include evangelism, teaching and deeds of mercy and compassion—in short, the entire ministry of the church to the entire world, beginning from Pentecost. These works are greater, not because they are more amazing miracles, but because they will be greater in their worldwide scope and will result in the transformation of individual lives and of whole cultures and societies.[139]

In John 15, Jesus presented Himself as the true vine who enables us, as the branches, to bear fruit and experience the fullness of His joy. He then proceeded to instruct His disciples in how they should relate to each other and to the world, which often expresses hatred for His followers. These teachings carry over into the opening verses of John 16, where our Lord reminds us of the promised Holy Spirit that He had already touched upon in the previous chapter (John 15:26). From there, He moves into His coming death and resurrection, leaving His disciples somewhat puzzled and bewildered. He closes the chapter with the unpleasant truth that they would face the prospect of tribulation so

---

[139] *ESV Study Bible*, 2052–2053.

long as they were in the world, although He assured them that He had already overcome the world.

The entirety of John 17 is devoted to the High Priestly Prayer of Christ, where He seems to break off abruptly from instructing His disciples in order to seek strength from His Heavenly Father to face the storm already upon Him. It is common for us to refer to Matthew 6:9–13 as the Lord's Prayer, but in reality this is the people's prayer, as Christ uses these familiar words to teach us how we ought to address our Heavenly Father. The true Lord's Prayer is found in John 17:1–26, where our Saviour prays for strength to embrace the shame and suffering that is even then beginning, and will end with His impalement on a Roman cross at a place called Golgotha.

In the Gospel of John, Christ speaks of God as the Father more than one hundred times, and in John 5 alone, He speaks of Himself as being sent from God six times consecutively (John 5:23–24, 30, 36–38).

Taking His disciples with Him, and traversing the same area where King David had walked and wept with his men many centuries before, the Lord Jesus crossed the Brook Kidron and entered the walled enclosure of the Garden of Gethsemane.[140] Kidron was an intermittent stream that was dry most of the year and became a raging torrent during the seasonal rains. The stream ran through the Kidron Valley, between the Temple Mount on the east of Jerusalem and the Mount of Olives farther east. The olive groves were home to many gardens, and according to Matthew 26:36 and Mark 14:32 this one was called Gethsemane, which means "oil press." From here, our Lord steeled Himself to embrace the cross upon which His purity and sinlessness would be violated by the wrath of a sinful world and where, for the sins of the world, He would bear the wrath of a holy God.[141]

This scene was soon followed by His betrayal by Judas, His appearance before the priests, Peter's denial, and His presentation to

[140] Compare John 18:1 with 2 Samuel 15:23, 30.

[141] Ibid., 567, 2060. See notations John 15:23–15:30 and John 18:1.

Pilate, the Roman governor of Judea, whose wife had warned him not to participate in any action against Christ (Matthew 27:19).

Inwardly torn by his own ambivalent feelings, but facing unrelenting pressure from the Jewish religious establishment, Pilate finally delivered Christ to the Roman soldiers for crucifixion, surely one of the most shameful and diabolical methods of execution ever devised by depraved humanity.

Following the death of Christ in John 19:30 comes a touching scene in which a secret disciple, Joseph of Arimathia, asked Pilate for the body of Jesus. Joseph was joined by Nicodemus, and these most unlikely of men were brought together to prepare the body of Christ for burial and to lay Him in a tomb where no one had yet been laid, indeed Joseph's own tomb, in fulfillment of Isaiah 53:9. Both men were intellectual, wealthy, influential, devout Jews, and believers, as is evidenced by their actions. Joseph of Arimathea appears in all four Gospels while Nicodemus appears only in John's Gospel.

The last two chapters of John are occupied with the empty tomb and several post-resurrection appearances of the Lord Jesus. The author had seen so much of the earthly ministry of Christ that he found it impossible to share all that he knew (John 21:25).

As we close out our comments on John's Gospel, I would like to point out several interesting observations.

Firstly, it wasn't Jewish custom to embalm the body of the departed, which helps explain John 11:39 in reference to Lazarus. The spices brought by Nicodemus were used to counteract the nauseating odours from decomposition of the body. It is estimated that Joseph and Nicodemus brought about sixty-five to one hundred pounds of mixed spices for the burial of Christ. They would have had to work quickly, because the Jewish Sabbath began at 6:00 p.m., sunset, when such labour had to cease. Their task was aided by the fact that the tomb was located near the place of crucifixion, an interesting piece of information that is recorded only by John (John 19:41–42).[142]

---

[142] Ibid., 1932. See notation John 15:46.

Secondly, certain details of the crucifixion produce some food for thought as we compare the four Gospel accounts. Many are unaware that not one of the Gospels tells of Jesus falling under the weight of the cross. Such is always assumed in books and movies about the crucifixion, but the Scriptures are silent.

The three synoptic Gospels record that the cross of Christ was carried by one Simon from Cyrene. Many assume that since Simon's country of origin was in northern Africa, he was a black African and probably a Gentile. What was Simon doing in Jerusalem at that time? The Bible account tells us that he came from the country and was picked at random from the crowd to be the cross-bearer of Christ. How did the Gospel writers know the name of this man? Mark records not only his name but the names of his two sons, Alexander and Rufus.

History records that Cyrene had a very large Jewish presence during the time of Christ, and the Jews were recognized as one of the four largest classes of people in Cyrene, whose government encouraged Jewish settlement. We also know that many of these Cyrenians had immigrated to the land of Israel, settling in and around the city of Jerusalem. They are referred to as one of the more significant people groups present in the day of Pentecost (Acts 2:10) and had their own synagogue in the city of Jerusalem (Acts 6:9).[143]

Simon may have been black as is commonly depicted, since he may have been of mixed race, but he could very well have been Jewish or at the very least a proselyte (Acts 2:10), which indicates a Gentile who has converted to the Jewish faith.

Matthew, Mark, and Luke do not give any indication that Christ ever carried His cross, let alone fell under its weight. Some Greek scholars point out that the construction of John 19:17 is open to question as to whether the phrase *"He, bearing his cross"* (NKJV) references Christ or someone else. Could this "He" refer to Simon of Cyrene and his name

[143] Merrill C. Tenney, ed., *Zondervan's Pictorial Bible Dictionary* (Grand Rapids, MI: Zondervan, 1967), 182–183.

was left out simply because John could not recall his name? It is known that John wrote long after the other Gospel writers. It is also known that many victims of crucifixion were simply unable to carry their cross because of the severe beatings inflicted on them beforehand.

Lastly, we note that Calvary is named only once in the Scriptures, in Luke 23:33. The name comes from the Latin, *Vulgate*, and comes from the same word as Golgotha. Contrary to every depiction of Calvary in books, movies, and hymns, there is no evidence that Calvary was located on a hill or even a steep incline. The Romans commonly crucified their victims along the main roads leaving or entering the towns and cities so as to serve as a warning to all who passed by. Indeed, it was against their better judgment to locate crosses on steep inclines in remote or hard-to-reach areas.

All we know from Scripture is that Calvary, or Golgotha, was just outside the city proper of Jerusalem. It was very conspicuous, probably near one of the city gates, located at the side of a highway, and it was near a garden that contained a tomb. A reasonable assumption is that the rock outcropping at Golgotha provided a backdrop to the crucifixion. The distance from Herod's palace to Golgotha was less than seven hundred feet. Notice carefully the wording in Matthew 27:39, where people passed by. Take note of Mark 15:21, where it says that Simon was passing by. Further compare Luke 23:33, 48–49, where the crowd came together to see the sight while the women who followed Him from Galilee stood at a distance.

The reference in John 19:20 tells us that the place of execution was near the city, with many Jews reading the inscription that Pilate had ordered to be placed on the cross. In John 19:25–26, some of Christ's family and others stood by the cross.

Every indication from these scriptures is that Christ was crucified near a well-travelled highway leading to and from Jerusalem, not on some remote high incline or hill in the country.

# The Acts of the Apostles

It is very possible that in the early days of the church, this historical document had no title. The extant Greek manuscripts available to us call this book Acts. The word was usually used to describe the achievements of great men, which certainly can be applied to this volume. The most prominent men in this book are Peter (Acts 1–12) and Paul (Acts 13–28). Some have suggested a more appropriate title for this account would be *The Acts of the Holy Spirit through the Apostles*, or the shortened title, *The Acts of the Holy Spirit.*

The book of Acts has the fingerprints of Luke all over it. From the earliest days of the church, there was never any reason to doubt his authorship of Acts. Along with the testimony of the early church fathers, internal evidence within the scriptures themselves are enough to establish Luke's penmanship. Both books are written to a man called Theophilus, who was identified in the introduction to Luke's Gospel as the high priest from 37–41 CE.

The first words of Acts refer to a former treatise, a former account, or more literally a former book which has obvious reference to the third

Gospel that Luke is credited with writing. There is such a close affinity between the closing verses of Luke's Gospel (Luke 24:45–53) with the opening verses of Acts (Acts 1:1–8) that even a casual reader could not miss the obvious connection of content, style, and format.

The two books fit perfectly together as two parts of the same historical and theological volume and express the thoughts of a single author. Luke's first book is summarized in the first verse of Acts, then the author continues into his second book without hesitation.

So closely do the two books dovetail together that some are convinced they were originally written as one volume at the same time by the same author. Thanks to men like Paul Barnett, we are now coming to have a fresh appreciation for what he and others refer to as Luke-Acts, seeing them as two parts of a whole. According to Barnett, "the former book narrated the works and words of Jesus and the second book narrated what He continued to do and say through His Spirit-filled apostles."[144]

Some modern writers are convinced that for too long we have elevated Paul's writings to such lofty heights that we've relegated the Gospels and Acts to a secondary level of importance for knowledge about the early days of the Christian faith. What needs to be appreciated is that while Paul had secondhand knowledge of the historical Jesus, Luke had firsthand knowledge, having been the recipient of material handed over to him by those who from the beginning had been eyewitnesses and ministers of the Word. Some have capably argued that the preface in Luke applies to both parts of his two-volume set. Evidence abounds that Luke incorporated written sources into his account (Acts 15:23–29, 23:26–30), perhaps interviewing some of the central leaders in the Jerusalem church, including Peter, John, and others.[145]

A careful reading of Acts shows that Luke was an eyewitness to many events recorded in Acts and was a frequent companion to the

---

[144] Paul Barnett, *The Birth of Christianity: The First Twenty Years* (Grand Rapids, MI: William B. Eerdmans Publishing, 2005), 190.

[145] Ibid., 192–194.

Apostle Paul as indicated by the "we" and "us" passages in his second volume (Acts 16:10–17, 20:5–21:18, 27:1–28:16).

Luke's writings are those of a meticulous researcher with an eye for detail, and a very knowledgeable historian who displays a rich knowledge of Roman laws and customs. His material also shows an intimate acquaintance with the geography of Palestine, Asia Minor, and Italy.

With the authorship of Acts firmly established, we now close this discussion with a discerning quote from Paul Barnett:

> In both volumes, we sense a connection with Old Testament salvation-history. God Himself is at work in both the earthly Jesus and the risen and ascended Jesus. Even in the more overtly historical second volume, the author is pressing the reader to confirm his commitment to the risen Lord. Nonetheless, the stated intention of both volumes makes Luke-Acts first and foremost a work of history.[146]

The Acts of the Apostles has twenty-eight chapters broken into:

- The Introduction (1:1–8)
- The Ascension (1:9–11)
- The Upper Room and Matthias (1:12–26)
- The Day of Pentecost (2:1–13)
- Peter's Sermon (2:14–36)
- The Church Grows (2:37–47)
- A Lame Beggar Healed (3:1–10)
- Peter's Second Sermon (3:11–26)
- Peter and John (4:1–37)
- Ananias and Sapphira (5:1–16)
- Imprisoned and Released (5:17–32)
- Gamaliel (5:33–42)

[146] Ibid., 196.

- The Seven (6:1–15)
- Stephen's Sermon and Death (7:1–60)
- Persecution (8:1–3)
- Philip and the Ethiopian (8:4–40)
- Conversion of Saul/Paul (9:1–31)
- Peter in Joppa (9:32–43)
- Cornelius and Peter (10:1–33)
- Gentiles hear the Gospel (10:34–48)
- Peter at Jerusalem (11:1–18)
- First Called Christians in Antioch (11:19–30)
- Peter's Arrest and Herod's Death (12:1–25)
- The First Missionary Journey (13:1–14:28)
- The Jerusalem Council (15:1–35)
- The Second Missionary Journey (15:36–18:22)
- The Third Missionary Journey (18:23–21:16)
- Paul in Jerusalem (21:17–23:22)
- Paul in Caesarea (23:23–26:32)
- Paul's trip to Rome (27:1–28:31)

## SUMMARY

It has been said that you are known by the company you keep. The author of Acts certainly kept good company, as he rubbed shoulders with some of the most influential personalities of the early church, not the least of these was the Apostle Paul, who became the driving force in the establishment of numerous local assemblies in the early part of the first century. Paul and Luke became travelling companions, evidenced by Paul's mention of Luke in three of his epistles written from prison (Colossians 2:14, 2 Timothy 4:11, Philemon 24).

Luke's second volume isn't just a history but a very selective history of the early church, which is essentially a history of salvation as the Holy Spirit moves well beyond the Jewish landscape into the far-flung enclaves of Gentile peoples everywhere. The spread of the Gospel from Jerusalem to Rome, and well beyond, was the fulfillment of the resurrected Christ's words to His apostles in Acts 1:8.

Though Acts is a moving and fast-paced account of the stupendous growth of the early church, it's also defined by its rich and varied theological content. There are thirty-two speeches in Acts which together constitute nearly a third of the total text. Of these addresses and sermons, ten could be considered of major significance. Three are attributed to Peter (Acts 2:14–36, 3:11–26, 10:34–43), one to Stephen (Acts 7:1–53), and six to Paul.

> Three of Paul's are defence speeches in Jerusalem and Caesarea (22:1–21; 24:10–21; 26:1–29). The other three consist of one speech on each of Paul's missionary journeys, each to a different type of assembly: to Jews on his first journey (13:16–47), to Gentiles on his second (17:22–31), and to Christians on his third (20:18–35). Much of the theological material of Acts is to be found in these speeches.[147]

Luke begins his second volume where his first ends, giving the reader a sense of continuity and connection that is kept fully intact when they're read back to back. Acts begins where all ministry should—in a prayer meeting, with this one held in the upper room where the disciples had met together with the Lord Jesus to eat the last Passover, and where Christ instituted the Lord's Supper. In this room, Jesus had told them that His betrayer was in their midst, and with the bread and cup He reminded them that He would soon shed His life's blood for the redemption of many. They then sang a song together, after which they made their way to the Mount of Olives (Mark 14:12–31).

In that same upper room in Acts 1, we see at least one hundred twenty people gathered together to do what Jesus asked them to do before His ascension: to wait in Jerusalem for the mighty outpouring of the Holy Spirit to empower them for service and soul-winning. With

---

[147] *ESV Study Bible*, 2075–2076.

the Apostle Peter taking the lead, they conduct a short business meeting in order to fill the apostolic vacancy that was created by the suicide of Judas Iscariot. Once they had narrowed the possible candidates down to two and spent time in prayer, they drew lots, whereupon Matthias became the twelfth apostle.

## THIS IS THAT

Before we collate the events that unfold in Acts 2, we need to reference the Old Testament Scriptures to which they are vitally connected. According to Leviticus 23, there were seven appointed feasts to which Jews were to assemble on an annual basis. This doesn't mean that all of Israel gathered in every case, but the three major feasts required all males of Israel to travel to the temple in Jerusalem (Exodus 23:14–19).

One such feast was the Feast of Weeks, also called the Feast of Harvest or The Feast of Pentecost. This feast was dedicated to the first fruits of the wheat harvest and occurred on the fiftieth day after the Sabbath (Leviticus 23:15–22, Exodus 23:16, Numbers 28:26–31, Deuteronomy 16:9–12). The wording of Leviticus 23:15–16 is very specific that the Jews were to number seven Sabbaths (forty-nine days), with the fiftieth day denoting the day of Pentecost.

The Jews of the New Testament era were very conversant in Greek and even had a Greek translation of the Old Testament called the Septuagint. From this version, we derive the word Pentecost, which is the Greek word for "fifty days" (Leviticus 23:16).

Flashforward to Acts 2:1, where those gathering in the upper room waited, as Jesus had instructed them. They were now at day fifty, and this *"was fully come"* (KJV) or *"had come"* (NASB). A more literal rendering of this phrase would be "was being fulfilled."

Picture this in your mind's eye: a group of Jews gathered in the upper room, which was probably located very near to the temple precinct, a sacred edifice to every Israelite. Many of us today, including

Roman Catholic scholar Ronald Knox, are more concerned with what went on there than with the location.

> The Upper Room must have been a cherished site for the disciples; A room haunted with memories-through that door did Judas slink out into the night, so short a time since; on that table the consecrated chalice reposed; through that window they listened to the shouts of "crucify him", that floor had been trodden by impassable feet. It was in these surroundings that the Holy Ghost visited his people on the day of Pentecost… the scene of their inspiration for the future was to be a scene enriched by past experience.[148]

The city of Jerusalem, and more especially the temple compound, was crowded to the max because every Jewish man, and many of their family members, had arrived for the fifty-day Feast of Weeks. Unlike any other Feast of Weeks that had come before, this one was to be the most memorable to all present. Gathered in the upper room were scores of people, including the disciples, the brothers of Christ, and His mother Mary.

Suddenly, there was a mighty rushing wind and the entire building was filled with a noise that had its source in heaven (Acts 2:2). The Old Testament had anticipated this many centuries before. All the offerings, ceremonies, festivals, and prophecies had looked forward to the Messiah for their fulfillment. God always had a plan, and on the day of Pentecost He arrived right on time.

Since this took place on the day after the seventh Sabbath, the Day of Pentecost occurred on a Sunday. Imagine how different our churches would be today if we could experience even a small fraction of what took place in that upper room during one of our typical Sunday morning services.

---

[148] Milton Walsh, *Ronald Knox as Apologist: Wit, Laughter, and the Polish Creed* (San Francisco, CA: Ignatius Press, 2007), 93–94.

As the tongues of fire fell and rested on each person, they experienced the fullness of the Holy Spirit and spoke with tongues as the Spirit prompted them. This homogenous group of Jews received such a baptism of God's Holy Spirit that all within their hearing, who had come from every corner of the Roman Empire, heard God's Word in their own dialect. Some questioned the whole episode while others made fun of them, accusing them of being in a drunken state (Acts 2:12–13)

When Peter stood up to preach in Acts 2:14, the words must have come effortlessly. After all, Peter and the others had just come off a fifty-day marathon of prayer followed by the greatest manifestation of God's presence and power in the history of the human race. Answering the critics, this impulsive but Spirit-filled fisherman assured his hearers that what they'd seen was a fulfillment of Old Testament prophecy. He quoted extensively from the book of Joel to support his message. I love the words of Acts 2:16, as given in the King James Version: *"But this is that which was spoken by the prophet Joel…"*

Peter's sermon and subsequent invitation yielded a harvest of three thousand souls. These early converts *"continued stedfastly in the apostles' doctrine and fellowship, and in breaking of bread, and in prayers"* (Acts 2:42, KJV).

## THE FILLING OF THE SPIRIT AND THE TONGUES CONTROVERSY

Over the years, there has been an ongoing discussion as to what figurative use of the term baptism is being utilized in Acts 1:5, previously predicted by John the Baptist in Matthew 3:11, and further promised by the Lord Jesus in Luke 24:49.

John Darby, C.I. Scofield, and others have argued that this baptism is that which is referenced in 1 Corinthians 12:13, which speaks of one becoming identified as part of the body of

Christ. While it could be capably argued by some that this is at least a part of the equation, others, including D.L. Moody, R.A. Torrey, and Charles Spurgeon, saw here an overwhelming endowment of power by the Holy Spirit that could be repeated many times. I concur with the latter.

What is called a baptism in Matthew 3:11 is referred to as an endowment with power in Luke 24:49, and further referenced as being baptized in the Holy Spirit in Acts 1:5. This same experience is described in Acts 2:4 as being filled with the Holy Spirit. Taking these verses together, we see that being baptized with the Holy Spirit is synonymous with being filled with the Holy Spirit. The same believers who were filled with the Holy Spirit in Acts 2:4 received another filling, or baptism, in Acts 4:31. Interestingly, nothing is said of tongues in the latter reference.

It is evident that the filling of Acts 2:4 isn't a one-time experience and can be repeated many times (Ephesians 5:18). In my opinion, this is not the "one baptism" of Ephesians 4:5, nor is it synonymous with the baptism into the body of Christ as expressed in 1 Corinthians 12:13. The filling of the Spirit is available to every believer and is rarely if ever evidenced by tongues (Luke 11:1–13).

Many sincere Christians have sought the so-called baptism evidenced by tongues and have been left disillusioned upon finding their most strenuous efforts to be in vain. Indeed, the most desperate of means is often utilized to enable Christians to experience tongues.

The filling of the Spirit in Acts 2:4 wasn't something new but had been experienced by some long before the day of Pentecost, including John the Baptist (Luke 1:15), Elisabeth (Luke 1:41), Zacharias (Luke 1:67), and Elijah (Luke 1:17). All scholars are agreed that something momentous and unusual took place on the day of Pentecost (Acts 2:4), but not all are agreed on its significance to the church at large. For the most part, dispensationalists are convinced that Pentecost signalled the beginning of a new era.

H.A. Ironside represents many when he wrote, "Pentecost was the beginning of a new age, that of the church, the body of Christ."[149] John R. Rice saw in this passage a major outpouring of God's power, but he states emphatically, "No new dispensation began at Pentecost. No different way of God's dealing with men began here."[150] Rice takes us back to John 20:19–22, strongly suggesting that too little attention has been given to what transpired before the day of Pentecost. He stresses,

> All these apostle and other Christians who waited at Pentecost for the enduement of power already had the Spirit of God dwelling within them. Whatever dispensational change there was in relation to the Holy Spirit occurred the day of the resurrection, not at Pentecost. The fullness of the Holy Spirit is not the same as the indwelling of the Spirit.[151]

Henry Morris states,

> All believers are baptized by the Holy Spirit into the body of Christ once for all at the time of conversion (1 Corinthians 12:13). They can, however, be filled [also called a baptism distinct from 1 Cor. 12:13] with the Spirit on more than one occasion and in fact, are exhorted to be [continually being] filled with the Spirit.[152]

---

[149] H.A. Ironside, *Acts* (Neptune, NJ: Loizeaux Brothers, 1960), 41.

[150] John R. Rice, *Acts of the Apostles* (Murfreesboro, TN: Sword of the Lord Publishers, 1963), 73.

[151] Ibid., 75.

[152] Morris, *The Henry Morris Study Bible*, 1630.

*The Expositor's Study Bible* stresses the permanence of the Holy Spirit in the hearts and lives of believers in Acts 2:4 but then adds a complication concerning the issue of speaking in tongues, suggesting that this is "the initial physical evidence that one has been baptized with the Spirit."[153]

With all due respect to my fellow believers who embrace this view, I would pose some questions. If one assumes that tongues is the initial evidence of Spirit baptism, how do we account for the numerous Christians who have never experienced speaking in tongues? Are they in a different category from the others? Does God bless some and withdraw his blessing from others?

An honest observation of Christians overall will reveal that only a part of the body of Christ makes a connection between baptism and tongues. For those readers who have been raised in a church that is Pentecostal or Charismatic in nature, I ask this question: do you consider your brothers and sisters who have never experienced tongues to be somehow inferior or deficient? How does this all square with 1 Corinthians 12:20–31?

Perhaps it's time for believers to have a serious conversation about an issue that has brought such confusion and division to the body of Christ.

One of the more helpful and objective commentators on the ramifications of Acts 2:4 is Rice, who explains the event of Pentecost in this fashion:

> Here is the key that explains all the terms used about what happened at Pentecost. When the disciples were "baptized with the Holy Ghost" as promised in Acts 1:5, they were simply surrounded, overwhelmed, submerged in the mighty power of God to enable them to witness. This is what it means to be "filled with the Holy Ghost", the more usual term, and more literal

[153] Swaggart, *The Expositor's Study Bible,* 1902.

> term used throughout the book of Acts, but referring to what happened at Pentecost in Acts 2:4. So to be filled with the Holy Spirit and to be baptized with the Spirit mean the same thing.[154]

This will not satisfy the standard dispensational view, which allows very little wiggle room in a boxed-in system, but it does seem to fit the biblical perspective. It will not satisfy those who insist that tongues must always accompany the baptism or filling of the Spirit, nor does the Word of God make such a demand.

Much misunderstanding has arisen over the reference to baptism in 1 Corinthians 12:13. We must be cautious about confusing the work of God with our carefully crafted theological system, which may or may not be fully in accord with the biblical model. We must allow the Word of God to speak freely, and we must not force the Word to speak only what we want to hear.

Much of Rice's teaching is very much in agreement with what many of us know as standard dispensational theology, but he never obligated himself to a preconceived system, only to the Scripture. His thoughts on Acts 2:4 and 1 Corinthians 12:13 are instructive:

> I think it is a mistake to confuse Acts 1:5, the promise that was fulfilled with these apostles on the day of Pentecost, with 1 Corinthians 12:13, which refers to the Christians at Corinth who were not even saved at Pentecost. No, baptized into the body of Christ by the agency of the Holy Spirit, which happens at conversion is one figure, and the floodtide or overwhelming enduement of power by the Holy Spirit for soul winning is another matter entirely.

---

[154] Rice, *Acts of the Apostles*, 50.

> There are two different figurative uses of the term baptism; baptized in the body of Christ and baptized in the Holy Ghost. The teaching of Darby, Kelly, and Scofield on the matter goes against the position of Moody, Torrey, Spurgeon and the other great teachers and soul winners. No, the baptism of the Holy Spirit in Acts 1:5 means the same as endued with power from on high in Acts 1:8, the same as filled with the Holy Ghost in Acts 2:4 and the gift of the Holy Ghost in Acts 2:38,39.[155]

Acts 5:14 records the phenomenal growth of the early church along with persecution that followed suit for centuries: "A Christian writer once summed it up this way: Christ's people in those early centuries 'out-thought, out-lived and out-died' their enemies in the Roman empire… by the year 300, there were Christians in every province of the Roman Empire."[156] Opposition didn't hinder the growth of the church but rather contributed to its increase in numbers.

One of the more celebrated early church fathers, Tertullian, was won to Christ by the public witness of martyrs.[157] This son of a centurion and one of the church's most accomplished theologians, was the first to coin the term Trinity to refer to God as Father, Son, and Spirit.[158] His description of church growth in North Africa at the end of the second century tells something of the many people who had come to Christ since the time of the apostles in the book of Acts: "We [i.e. Christians] are but

---

[155] Ibid., 37–38.

[156] Perry Thomas, *Exploring Church History* (Nashville, TN: World Publishing, 2005), 14.

[157] M. Cary and H.H. Scullard, *A History of Rome* (London, UK: McMillan Press, 1979), 35, 39–40.

[158] Lang, *1001 Things…*, 268.

of yesterday [i.e. newcomers] and we have filled all you have-cities, islands, forts, towns, assembly-halls, even military camps, tribes, town councils, the palace, Senate, and forum. We have left you nothing but the temples."[159]

The teaching that new converts should wait and seek for a baptism evidenced by tongues has only been taught in more recent times, with the advent of the Pentecostal movement. By their own admission, many of the Pentecostal persuasion have never received their so-called baptism. Perhaps someone can answer this lingering question: why not? To those who embrace this teaching, we ask how this squares with Romans 8:32 and 1 Corinthians 2:12. God is a God of grace and He doesn't have favourites in His church. With some, the tongues phenomenon has become an unnatural obsession which takes precedence over holiness of life and soul-winning.

## PENTECOSTALISM: A BRIEF HISTORY

The present-day Pentecostal movement can be traced back to the early morning hours of the first day of the twentieth century. Reportedly, preacher and teacher Charles Parham of Topeka, Kansas laid his hands on the head of Agnes Ozman, who almost immediately began to speak in tongues. Others soon began to experience the same and it soon became popular to seek the gift of tongues.

This became the catalyst for the Azusa Street revival of 1906 in Los Angeles, led by William Seymour, an African American who told his parishioners that the evidence of the baptism of the Holy Spirit was tongues, not sanctification. It could be debated whether Seymour was the first to coin the phrase "baptism of the Spirit evidenced by tongues." What is known, by his own admission, is that Seymour's theology of tongues came from Charles Parham, the person who is often credited

[159] Cary and Scullard, *A History of Rome*, 486.

with the baptism evidenced by tongues terminology. Perhaps the expression was used earlier, but there is little evidence of such. It was the movement spawned by Parham and Seymour that most certainly popularized it.[160]

The Pentecostal churches that evolved from the early twentieth century established their own denominational entity, but in more recent years this movement has touched many other denominations, including the Roman Catholic Church. Now known as the Charismatic movement, it is very nearly synonymous with Pentecostalism.

Mystical stirrings from the more distant past remind us of the Pentecostalism of today, but they were of short duration. They include the Zwickau prophets of the sixteenth-century Reformation who boasted of visions, dreams, and direct communication with God.[161]

There is perhaps no individual in church history who more represents the Charismatic movement of today than Presbyterian minister Edward Irving of Scotland. Born in 1792, it appears that Irving didn't employ the phrase "baptism evidenced by tongues," but ecstatic utterances, healing, and prophecy were all key components in his ministry. Forced from his church in 1833, Irving and his followers organized a new fellowship, the Catholic Church. Broken and discouraged, Irving passed on the following year.[162]

Largely ignored by history for far too long, researchers in more recent times have come to recognize Irving and the church he founded to be a precursor of the modern-day Charismatic movement.

---

[160] Hank Hanegraaff, *Counterfeit Revival* (Dallas, TX: Word Publishing, 1997), 125–127.

[161] Philip Schaff, *History of the Christian Church, Volume 7* (Peabody, MA: Hendrickson Publishers, 2006), 381.

[162] McGovern, ed., *Chambers Biographical Dictionary*, 781.

> That is, during his last five years his doctrinal position was virtually that of the Pentecostal body of today. He believed God was then granting a restoration of the Apostolic gifts, especially those of "tongues", "healing" and "prophecy", and his views were such that, although he preceded our day by a century and a half, he well deserved the recognition he has recently begun to receive: "The fore-runner of the Charismatic Movement."[163]

Influenced by A.J. Scott and McLeod Campbell, Edward Irving believed that those who spoke in tongues (those who received the baptism) were superior to those who didn't.[164] This view, whether in reality or perceived, is to my mind the major weakness in the modern-day Pentecostal movement, just as it was then.

The empowerment to win souls is paramount in the book of Acts, where thousands were swept into the kingdom of God. According to the New Testament, especially in the books of Ephesians and 1 Corinthians, all believers are on equal footing before God. The power of the Holy Spirit is available to every believer, enabling us to live a life that exhibits the fruit of the Spirit (Galatians 5:22) and bring the unsaved to Christ (Acts 2:37–43).

The unifying factor for believers is a personal relationship with the Lord Jesus Christ (1 Corinthians 10:17). The party spirit and comparison complex are soundly renounced in 1 Corinthians 1:10, 3:3–5, 4:6–7 and 2 Corinthians 10:12. Placing undue emphasis on one aspect of truth to the near exclusion of all others is lopsided theology.

There also lingers a very strong and uncomfortable feeling that those among us who have never experienced tongues will

---

[163] Arnold Dallimore, *The Life of Edward Irving: The Forerunner of the Charismatic Movement* (Carlisle, PA: The Banner of Truth Trust, 1983), ix.

[164] Ibid., 177.

never measure up to or be fully accepted as equals by some who claim to have had the same experience as believers on the day of Pentecost.

Romans 8 has been described by some as a detailed and rich commentary on the abundance of life that Christ came to give to all who would trust Him as Saviour and Lord (John 10:10). The Holy Spirit is named repeatedly as Paul reminds us of all what we have in Christ. Romans 8:9–11 makes clear that every believer is indwelt by the Holy Spirit, who also bears witness that we are the children of God (Romans 8:16).

In the thirty-nine verses of Romans 8, the manifestation of tongues and other sign-gifts are absent from the discussion. All Christians are seen as being foreknown, predestined, called, justified, and glorified (Romans 8:29–30). The door is effectively slammed shut against any who would even hint that only their brand of Christianity is acceptable before God, being superior to all others. Consider Romans 12:3:

> *For I say, through the grace given unto me, to every man that is among you, not to think of himself more highly than he ought to think; but to think soberly, according as God hath dealt to every man the measure of faith.* (KJV)

The issue of tongues has been given an exalted status by some, a status that goes far beyond the mandate of Scripture. It is mentioned only once in the Gospels, five times in the book of Acts, and only in one of Paul's epistles, and there it is severely abused, requiring firm restrictions on its use in the local church. It has become a source of pride and division that has needlessly alienated Christians from each other and brought confusion to worship services. Giving the impression that we have more than our fellow Christians, or that we are somehow more spiritual because we have spoken in tongues, is foreign to the spirit of Christian faith.

Following the healing of the lame beggar, Peter preached a second sermon in Acts 3. This was followed by a period of intense persecution during which Peter and John were arrested, threatened, and then released.

The evident disparity between rich and poor is addressed by the early church in Acts 4:32–37, with many believers selling homes and land and then giving all the received funds to the apostles for appropriate distribution. One such individual was Ananias, who in collusion with his wife Sapphira sold a piece of real estate, then brought only a part of the purchase price to the apostles. The deception was quickly spotted by the Apostle Peter, and as a warning to others discipline was swiftly carried out. After being strongly rebuked, Ananias and Sapphira died within three hours of each other.

With increasing persecution of the church coming from a zealous Jewish population, one of their own, a Pharisee and teacher of the Law by name of Gamaliel, pleaded for cooler head to prevail (Acts 5:33–42). We learn later, in Acts 22:3, that Gamaliel had taught the Apostle Paul.

Acts 6 tells of seven men who were chosen to address some of the more mundane aspects of ministry among the Hellenistic Jews who felt neglected. One of these men, Stephen, was gifted with miraculous powers (Acts 6:8) and a riveting preacher of the Gospel (Acts 7). So intense was the opposition to his ministry that he was put to death by stoning (Acts 7:54–60). In the minds of some, he was the first recorded Christian martyr in the New Testament. Although some would insist, as does this author, that this description best fits John the Baptist.

Acts 7:58 introduces us to a man named Saul, who was a major leader of Jewish efforts to stifle the rapid growth and widening influence of the early church.

One of the more prominent leaders of the evangelistic effort in Samaria was Philip, who along with Stephen was numbered with the seven mentioned in Acts 6:5. On Philip's way back to Jerusalem, an angel directed him to take the road to Gaza whereupon he happened upon a eunuch from Ethiopia who was busily engaged in the reading of the prophet Isaiah. From this Old Testament scripture, Philip led the man, a state official, to Christ and baptized him.

Acts 9 tells of the stirring conversion of Saul, soon to be known as the Apostle Paul, on the road to Damascus. He began to preach Christ almost immediately in Damascus and was soon in danger of being put to death by the unbelieving Jews.

The next chapters tell of how Peter, after seeing a vision, learned an important lesson that the Gospel of Christ was meant for both Jews and Gentiles.

The truth that God is impartial and extends His grace and mercy to all unconditionally was further strengthened by the conversion of a man called Cornelius in Caesarea. This Roman centurion became the first Gentile convert, providing a vivid illustration of God's intention to reap a harvest of souls among the Gentiles as well as the Jews.

Peter then gave a report to the Christians in Jerusalem informing them that God's love and forgiveness was to be freely extended to the Gentiles. Attention was then given to the growth of the church in Antioch where the disciples were first called Christians, an appellation that has survived to the present day (Acts 11:26).

The death of James, the brother of John, is recorded in Acts 12:2 and is followed by the imprisonment of Peter. There is exciting reading here as Peter was miraculously released from prison, and to the amazement of all he ended up at a prayer meeting being held on his behalf.

The details of Herod's violent death in Acts 12:20–23 remind us anew of God's absolute sovereignty over the affairs of men.

With much of the persecution against the church ending with Herod's passing, the church continued to grow and entered into a new era. The focus of the book turns from Peter, whose ministry had overshadowed all others up to this point, to the Apostle Paul, whose massive influence on the church is nothing short of astonishing.

Luke's narrative depicts the rapid growth of the early church, we are soon introduced to a variety of fascinating personalities and varied geographical locales that are so very familiar to us from the annals of ancient history. Luke's writings are a constant reminder that the people, places, and events of Acts are far more than pieces of information for the curious observer, information that, to some minds, may have little to no relevance to the church of the twenty-first century. He employs masterful literary skills to acquaint us with what the Lord Jesus predicted in John 14:12, the church's extension to the far corners of the Roman Empire and beyond. Empowered by the Holy Spirit and undeterred by the most violent of persecution, the early Christians continued to multiply and expand their influence to every race and culture.

The two-volume document left to us by Luke the beloved physician doesn't end with Paul's imprisonment in Rome. Rather, it is still being written across the world in the hearts of millions who become part of God's kingdom (Luke 17:21). The historical and spiritual odyssey that plays itself out in time, and which is still ongoing, finds its source in the heart of God. Acts should be read against the backdrop of Ephesians 3:1–7, where the church is no longer seen as a hidden mystery but a living, growing, and vibrant body in full view, a trophy of God's grace for all eternity. The mystery is not so much a church hidden in ages past; the church now is one body encompassing both Jews and Gentiles.

The study of Acts will be greatly enriched as we take the time to peruse the maps found at the back of most Bibles. It will also be helpful to access a Bible dictionary or the notes in a good study Bible to better acquaint ourselves with the many towns and places that are named in Luke's narrative.

From Acts 13:1 to the end of the book, the travels of Paul are paramount. Four missionary journeys are recorded of Paul and his companions, although some scholars would argue there was a fifth, to

Spain, which was never recorded. From Acts 16:10–28:16, Luke often identifies himself with the company of Paul, which means our writer was an eyewitness to many of the events recorded in his narrative.

The Apostle Paul is initially brought to our attention in Acts 7:58 when the robes of Stephen's murderers are laid at his feet. Perhaps this was when Saul of Tarsus (Acts 9:11) first began to feel the pangs of conviction that would lead to his moving conversion on the road to Damascus. When we read the words of Paul in Colossians 1:24–29, in which he shares the heart of his calling, it is hard to imagine that in the past he had so hated and ravaged the church of which he was now the most influential leader.

The remaining chapters of Acts are essentially a summary of the travels, travails, and triumphs of the man whom even some secular historians refer to as the greatest force in European history for more than two thousand years. Before entering Acts 13, we will here delineate Paul's four missionary journeys, as given by Luke:

- The First Missionary Journey (Acts 13:1–14:28)
- The Second Missionary Journey (Acts 15:39–18:22)
- The Third Missionary Journey (Acts 18:22–21:16)
- The Fourth Missionary Journey (Acts 27:1–28:16)

Acts 13 marks a turning point. While the first twelve chapters are focused on the growth of the church in Jerusalem and Judea under the leadership of Peter, the attention now turns to the spread of the Gospel throughout the Roman world under the leadership of Paul.

Except for the city of Jerusalem, no other city in the ancient world experienced more Christian activity than did Antioch (now called Antakya) in the southeastern part of modern-day Turkey. This city became the location of the first Gentile church and it was here that many Christians fled during the martyrdom of Stephen. When Jerusalem was stricken with famine, the Christians of Antioch sent relief supplies, entrusting their delivery to Paul and Barnabas.

Paul was brought from his home in Tarsus by Barnabas and together they were occupied with teaching and encouraging the church in Antioch for a full year. It was also here that trouble brewed as Jewish converts began to pressure the Gentiles to submit to the Jewish rite of circumcision. This became the catalyst for the Council of Jerusalem, which was called in Acts 15 (Acts 11:19–30, 15:1–2).

Upon the return of Paul and Barnabas to Antioch from their mission to Jerusalem (Acts 11:30), they were accompanied by a man called John Mark, a cousin to Barnabas (Acts 12:12, Colossians 4:10), who would soon be a source of tension. This Mark became the author of the Gospel that bears his name (Acts 12:25).

## PAUL'S FIRST MISSIONARY JOURNEY

The first foreign missions trip in history, excepting Jonah's voyage to the Assyrians more than eight hundred years earlier, was undertaken when this threesome made their way from Antioch to the seaport of Seleucia. From there, they set sail for Cyprus, which was the home of Barnabas and had a large Jewish population. From their landing in Salamis, they proceeded to the capital city of Paphos, where they encountered a sorcerer called Elymas and witnessed the conversion of a Roman official. They then sailed northwest to Perga, in the Roman province of Pamphylia, bordered by the Taurus Mountains. There, John Mark left the scene and returned to Jerusalem.

Paul and Barnabas pushed north to Antioch of Pisidia, where at first they were well received by the large Jewish presence. In Acts 13:14–15, Paul and Barnabas found themselves in the Jewish synagogue on the Sabbath, and following an open invitation to address the gathering Paul preached a stirring and well-received Gospel message (Acts 13:16–41).

By the arrival of the next Sabbath, nearly the entire city had descended upon the synagogue to hear these visiting evangelists. In the face of such a positive response from the Gentile populace, the Jews vented their rage against Paul and Barnabas and began to revile them.

Acts 13:46 marks a major turning point, not only for Paul's ministry but for the church at large. The missionary duo made a decision not to continue giving their message primarily to the Jews, which had been their practice, but to now concentrate their efforts on the Gentiles. Pointing to Isaiah 42:6, Paul and Barnabas reminded their countrymen that they'd been responsible from the beginning to take the good news to the Gentiles, but all was to no avail. By the end of the chapter, they are forced out of the city and make their way to Iconium.

The ruins of Antioch of Pisidia lie near the town of Yalvac in modern Turkey. Scholars have long debated just how long Paul and Barnabas remained there following their rejection by the Jewish quarter, with some suggesting their expulsion may have been prolonged. Regardless, Paul's ministry took on a different complexion as he focused primarily on the large masses of Gentiles rather than on his own privileged people. In the city of Iconium, just southeast of Antioch of Pisidia, their reception was little better, and after being threatened with stoning by an unruly mob of Jews and Gentiles they fled to Lystra.

## THE UNFINISHED SERMON

One would think that having been threatened and harassed, barely escaping with their lives in their last two stopovers, things couldn't possibly get any worse, but trouble frequently follows trouble.

The campaign in Lystra, just a short distance south of Iconium, seemed to get off to a good start. These travel-weary evangelists had the freedom to preach and received a most positive reception. But we can be well assured that whatever Paul hoped for at the end of his sermon in Acts 14:7, it was a far different outcome than what he or Barnabas realized.

An unplanned interruption during Paul's speech caused the wheels to come off this evangelistic endeavour. Among the people who were listening with rapt attention was a man who had been lame from his mother's womb. As he listened to this converted Jew and fixed his eyes upon him, he caught the attention of Paul (Acts 14:8–9). The sermon was brought to a screeching halt when Paul shouted loudly for the lame man to stand to his feet. The man leaped up and walked in sheer delight—and the crowd took notice. That's when everything fell apart.

## CHAOS IN LYSTRA

Perhaps due to a language barrier, or simply bewildered by the mass hysteria among the people, Paul and Barnabas seemed stunned by what took place before their eyes. After a brief hesitation, they realized that the miracle of healing had convinced these people that their gods, Zeus and Hermes, had come down to visit them in the human forms of Paul and Barnabas. To the utter amazement of the evangelists, the people were preparing to offer sacrifices and honour them as gods. With wild gesturing and loud protestations, Paul and Barnabas were scarcely able to restrain the masses and persuade them not to offer sacrifices to them.

This is all played out for us in Acts 14:11–18, but the passage is far from finished, as we shall now see.

What more could happen to Paul and his associate while preaching in Lystra? Just when they thought they had the crowd under control, when they had convinced them that they weren't Greek gods incarnate, another troubling situation developed on the southern highway from Iconium. As Paul and Barnabas became engrossed in a verbal exchange with the residents of Lystra, an angry mob of Jews from the cities of Antioch and Iconium entered the outer fringes of the city and began persuading the fickle masses to join forces with them to settle the score with Paul and Barnabas once and for all.

We aren't certain from Acts 14:19 what happened to Barnabas, but Paul was stoned and left for dead.

What happened next is nothing short of incredible. After they dragged Paul outside the city, he suddenly got up and re-entered the city that had just thrown him out. There are obvious details missing from the account, but the next day Paul and Barnabas exited the city and headed for Derbe.

Some argue that Paul actually died at Lystra and was raised from the dead, but to me this is just fanciful thinking (Acts 14:19–20); he was obviously stunned by the attack and fell unconscious for a time, but there is no evidence that he died. He almost certainly was healed from any life-threatening injuries, and the day after the attack he was able to leave the city, apparently in good health, which in itself was a miracle.

You would think by now that these harried and persecuted evangelists would take the fast train home, but they didn't. Luke is careful to remind us that they reaped a large harvest of souls in Derbe, after which they backtracked to all three cities that had treated them so miserably and organized churches in each one (Acts 14:21–23). From there, they made the return trip to Antioch of Cilicia, where they had started. The timeframe for this journey was AD 46–48.

## THE JERUSALEM COUNCIL

The second missionary journey was delayed for a time while some of the great Christian leaders of the day gathered in Jerusalem for the first and perhaps greatest council to be held during the infant days of the church.

Among the keynote speakers for this important gathering were the Apostle Peter and James, brother of the Lord Jesus. The issue to be settled had to do with the essentials of the Gospel. They had to answer this question for all eras of the church: "What must I do to be saved? What are the minimum requirements?" The Jewish converts insisted that Gentiles embrace the rite of circumcision, but this requirement was rejected by the Jerusalem council.

Following an address by Peter, the final summation was given by James, the senior pastor in Jerusalem. We could rightly assume that James presided over this historic gathering and, using the wisdom he talks of in the book he authored (James 1:5, 3:13–18), gave his final judgment with a letter sent to all the churches to communicate that decision.

Acts 15:1–29 deals with the plan and procedure of the Jerusalem council. With the council concluded, Paul and Barnabas took their letter and returned to Antioch to prepare for another missionary enterprise.

## A HEATED EXCHANGE

Preparations for a second journey into Asia Minor got off to a rather rocky start. According to Acts 15:36–39, Paul and Barnabas found themselves embroiled in a major disagreement over the inclusion of John Mark. The insistence by Barnabas that Mark be included was vigorously rejected by Paul. The language of Acts 15:39 suggests that this was no minor tiff over a coffee at Tim Horton's, but rather a long, protracted, emotional exchange that ended with the two men unable to find common ground.

Finally, Barnabas took Mark and headed for his home on Cyprus while Paul took Silas and departed to Syria and Cilicia. It is quite likely that Paul then began his second journey by visiting churches he had founded before settling into Antioch. We also know from Galatians 1:21 that the circumcision issue had been raised in the areas of Syria and Cilicia.

Some Bible scholars believe that Paul's first venture into Asia Minor may have been cut short and that his initial plans had been to cover a much wider area which would have entailed a much longer timeframe. There were also the personality clashes that seemed to intensify with John Mark's departure from Paul and Barnabas at Perga. This situation continued to fester and was the fly in the ointment that forced these strong personalities to travel in different directions at the outset of the second journey.

Even in the face of schism, God is never frustrated and can use the most awkward of moments for His own glory.

As Paul set out on his second journey, this time with a different associate, we reach yet another turning point. In Acts 16, we will see how God diverted Paul's attention from Asia to Europe, something for which we in Canada and the United States should be everlastingly grateful, since our countries are the offspring of European civilization.

At the outset of Acts 16, Paul and Silas visited two of the cities where he had founded churches on his initial journey, Derbe and Lystra. No doubt Paul was fully reminded of his harrowing experience at the latter city, but this time he returned in relative calm.

Once in Lystra, Paul and Silas made the acquaintance of a young man by the name of Timothy whose mother was a Jew and his father a Greek (Gentile). Timothy was a believer and already showed signs of leadership qualities.

Wanting Timothy to join them in their travels, Paul had him circumcised (Acts 16:3). Some see this as a compromise on Paul's part, but I think not. The rite continued his Jewish connection on his mother's side of the family, giving him acceptance by the Jews as well as access to synagogues.

As Paul and his party left Lystra, they continued to distribute letters to the churches which had been drafted at the Jerusalem council.

## EVANGELISM IN EUROPE

For reasons unknown to Paul at the time, he was denied access to the cities of Asia by divine intervention (Acts 16:6).

Paul and his workers finally arrived at Troas, located just a short distance from the ancient city of Troy. Ruins of this city still survive, but this area at Daylan in modern-day Turkey has been deserted and left to the elements.

From here, Paul received a vision in the night of a man from Macedonia calling for help, and without any hesitation he and his contingent set sail for Samothrace and Neapolis.

It seems that Luke joined with Paul's company at Troas, which is indicated by the switch of pronouns from "they" to "we."[165] Having landed on the continent of Europe, Paul and his party went directly to the city of Philippi. Named after Philip of Macedon, father to Alexander the Great, who had conquered it in 360 BC, it was the leading city of Macedonia, and in Paul's time part of a Roman colony.

Their first convert was a woman of means named Lydia who had moved there from the city of Thyatira. This first European Christian saw all of her household converted to Christ and her home became a haven for Paul and his fellow workers (Acts 16:15–40).

They saw some harassment from a fortuneteller, but Paul delivered her from the grip of a demon. When her former employers saw that she was no longer of use to them for financial gain, they incited a riot that resulted in the imprisonment of Paul and Silas. Following their miraculous escape, their jailer and his entire family came to Christ.

After a brief respite at Lydia's home, they made their way to Thessalonica, where they were accosted by an angry mob and had to escape under the cover of darkness (Acts 17:10) to Berea. It seems that Luke had now detached himself from Paul's company again, as is evidenced by the use of "they" once more. He then rejoined them in Acts 20:5–21:18 and 27:1–28:16.

They had great success in Berea, with some of the prominent citizens coming to Christ, but Paul's troubles were far from over as some of the more antagonistic Jews arrived from Thessalonica to stir up the Bereans against Paul (Acts 17:13). Fearing for Paul's safety, the believers in Berea whisked him out of the city and, under escort, on to Athens.

Heading south, Paul would not have failed to see Mount Olympus, which due to its past glories still provides inspiration for the modern-day Olympic movement.

Angered by the wholesale idolatry in Athens and observing an altar dedicated to a god they didn't know, Paul positioned himself on Mars

[165] Compare Acts 16:8 with Acts 16:10.

Hill (Areopagus) and preached one of the most moving and powerful sermons in the history of the church.

Acts 18:1–3 finds Paul leaving the cultured city of Athens and moving on to the city of Corinth, where he made the acquaintance of Aquila and his wife Priscilla. They had been part of a forced expulsion of Jews from Italy and had recently settled in Corinth, a thriving trading centre with two busy harbours. This Christian couple was in the tent-making trade, as was Paul (Acts 18:3), and during his eighteen-month stay in Corinth he stayed at their home.

With Aquila and Priscilla in tow, Paul travelled to Ephesus, the most prominent city in Asia Minor.

Leaving the two tentmakers in Ephesus, Paul began the final leg of his journey. Before hastily leaving the city that Pliny called "the ornament of Asia," Paul dropped into the synagogues for a brief encounter with the Jewish leaders (Acts 18:19). According to the next verse, Paul was well received—so much so that they strongly entreated him to extend his visit. But for reasons that aren't clearly spelled out for us, Paul was in a hurry to be on his way.

According to Paul's own words, it wasn't his intention to go straight home to Antioch but to make a beeline to Jerusalem in order to attend a feast, possibly the Feast of Passover. It may have been Paul's intention to mingle with his countrymen from all over the empire, including Christians who might be visiting the city at that same time.

We also read Paul's vow, taken at Cenchrea, an outport of Corinth, to shave his head. This was based on the Nazirite vow in the Old Testament (Numbers 6:2, 5, 13–15). It was common for early church Jewish Christians to use this vow as a pledge of separation and devotion to God. Once the hair was shaved off, it was kept, and within thirty days the devotee had to present his shorn head to the people at the temple and present the hair as a gift. This may have been another factor that prompted Paul's insistence on getting to David's city with due haste.

The timeframe for this second journey was AD 49–52.

## UP OR DOWN?

Whatever the reason, Paul resisted all efforts to have him tarry in Ephesus. But according to Acts 18:21, he assured the people of Ephesus that he would, God willing, make a return visit to their city.

Some struggle with the exact of meaning of Acts 18:22, which says in the King James Version, *"And when he had landed in Caesarea, and gone up, and saluted the church, he went down to Antioch"* (KJV). While reading this verse, it's helpful to access a map that shows Paul's movements on his second journey. Keep in mind that Luke and his early church readers knew their geography far better than many modern-day readers and they would not be puzzled, as we are, with the intent of this verse.

Observing Acts 18:21, we note that Paul sailed from Ephesus. Rounding the southwestern tip of modern-day Turkey, his ship sailed straight for Caesarea, which took them just off the southwestern tip of Cyprus. They may have stopped at Paphos for supplies before continuing. This was a common trade route in Paul's day.

The port city of Caesarea was located just northwest of the city of Jerusalem, and though that city isn't named we know from Acts 18:21 that this was Paul's destination. The church mentioned here is the church in Jerusalem, but how can one go *up* when you're travelling south?

The Greek language is explicit here and there is no room for a variant reading. The answer lies in the geography of Israel. Jerusalem is on a much higher elevation than the land that surrounds it, which means you must go *up* to the city even from the northern region.

This further explains the last part of the verse, which says that Paul went *down* to Antioch, which was due north of Jerusalem.

We usually think of going *up* as heading north, but as Paul left Jerusalem he went *down*, even though travelling north, because the elevation kept dropping as he made his way home.

## MIGHTY IN THE SCRIPTURES

Once in Antioch, Paul made plans for another venture, but he probably spent the winter in the city, which takes us into the spring of AD 53.

From Luke's description in Acts 18:23, we learn that Paul initiated his third journey by taking the land route northwest from Antioch, and with determination to fulfill a promise made the previous year he set his sights on Ephesus. It is unfortunate that the chapter division in our Bibles comes at the end of Acts 18:28 rather than at the end of Acts 18:22, because the last six verses of the chapter are vitally connected to the chapter that follows.

In Acts 18:23–28, Luke introduces us to a man called Apollos, born among the Jews in Alexandria, Egypt. He had obviously been converted and now preached the Gospel of Christ in Ephesus, knowing only John's baptism. He was very proficient in his knowledge of the Old Testament, so much so that he is the only man in the Bible to be described as *"mighty in the scriptures"* (Acts 18:24, KJV). He had an accurate knowledge of the life of Christ, which he may have learned from an early written Gospel or from Galilean Christians who may have drifted over to Alexandria from Palestine.

To be sure, there were deficiencies in his theological framework, but they were corrected by the patient understanding and instruction of Aquila and Priscilla. He seems to have had little or no knowledge of the outpouring of the Holy Spirit or the rite of Christian baptism, such as is found in the last few verses of Matthew's Gospel.

By the time we arrive at Acts 19:1, Apollos, in accordance with his request in Acts 18:27, had crossed the Aegean Sea and settled in Corinth in Achaea, where his ministry evidently prospered (Acts 18:27–28).

Meanwhile, Paul had arrived in Ephesus, where he found a group of men who exhibited some of the same theological weaknesses as did Apollos before he'd become acquainted with Aquila and Priscilla. The King James Version refers to them as *"certain disciples"* (Acts 19:1).

## ENCOUNTER AT EPHESUS

The three-year ministry of the Apostle Paul in Ephesus, laid out for us in Acts 19:1–41, is prefaced by Paul's encounter with twelve men as he first enters the city on his second and extended visit. The account in Acts 19:1–7 has been the subject of much theological wrangling and ongoing controversy, especially since the advent of the dispensational approach to the Scriptures in the early 1800s, as well as the more recent Charismatic movement over the last one hundred years.

The incident of Acts 19:1–7 took place twenty-five years after the martyrdom of John the Baptist and more than twenty years after the day of Pentecost. Ephesus was over six hundred miles from Palestine, which tells me that they never saw John the Baptist. It's also clear from Acts 19:2 that they knew nothing about the day of Pentecost and the outpouring of the Holy Spirit. This is pointed out by S.E. Anderson, who quotes John A. Broadus: "It was evident that when they previously received baptism (probably from some ignorant disciple of John) it had been without knowledge what they were about."[166]

Anderson then carries his argument to another level. "Further, Acts 19:4 seems to imply that these 12 men had never heard the real Gospel of Christ. When Paul instructed them in the essentials of salvation, then they were properly baptized."[167]

---

[166] S.E. Anderson, *Baptists Unshackled* (Glenwood, IL: Fundamental Baptist Press, 1971), 34.

[167] Ibid., 35.

Since Luke was writing of this after the fact and didn't rejoin Paul until Acts 20:5, in what context did he see these men as disciples? Does this refer to them when Paul first meets them or after their conversion and subsequent baptism? I suggest that he referred to their state in the latter.

In Acts 19:2, we see Paul ask a very casual but straightforward question in order to extract information. He wasn't laying down a formula as to how the Holy Spirit was to be received but only probing for a response. The question comes immediately, but you can be sure there was some preliminary discussion between Paul and these men before he unloaded the question on them. Paul was a well-educated man and would not ask such a thing without investigating these men's spiritual state. From their answer, Paul learned of their total ignorance of God's Holy Spirit.

In my mind, our modern English translators have replaced the word *since* with the word *when* in order to fortify a predetermined theological system of thought about the Holy Spirit. Modern translators believe this is a more accurate rendering, but it does little to clarify the text.

Here is my paraphrase and expansion of Paul's question in order to catch the force of his inquiry: "Now that you have shared with me your profession of belief, I want to know what experience you have had with the Holy Spirit since that time."

I would argue that the translators of 1560 and 1611 caught the full impact of what Paul was asking. He already knew they weren't true believers and that their belief system was virtually non-existent, but he pushed them to verbalize what he already suspected. The question is thrown out casually not to prove a theological point but to test the genuineness of their belief.

Their reply came quickly and to the point: they hadn't heard of the Holy Spirit and they knew nothing about His work, power, and ministry. Their ignorance betrayed their emptiness of knowledge and experience with God.

In Acts 19:3, Paul followed up their answer with another bated question. Their preliminary conversation told him they had been baptized, and now he asked about their baptism and belief. Again I offer a paraphrase of Paul's question: "What does your baptism mean to you and by whose authority was it performed?"

When they heard this, they were baptized in the name of the Lord Jesus. Like Apollos, they had been baptized into John's baptism by one of John's disciples, but unlike Apollos, they knew nothing about the Lord Jesus or about the repentance required before water baptism was to be embraced.

With their limited knowledge and obvious lack of true conversion evident, Paul shared the Gospel with them in Acts 19:4. We can be sure that much more was said than Luke gives us in his narrative, but we are able to glean the gist of the message. Paul didn't fail to remind them that John's baptism was not a formality but rather a rite to be seriously undertaken only after one had truly repented of sin and professed a saving faith in the Lord Jesus Christ. These prerequisites are mandatory for water baptism to have any meaningful significance.

These men were obviously open for the message of the Gospel, as they were baptized in Acts 19:5. This doesn't mean that John's initial baptism was invalid, but it was a necessity for these men because they had been previously baptized with no knowledge of salvation through Christ. They also would have known about the work of the Holy Spirit had they been exposed to John's preaching, as he spoke no less than six times in the Scriptures about the work of the Holy Spirit. Whoever had baptized them earlier had no knowledge of salvation or they would have shared such with these men.

While the men Paul engaged as he entered Ephesus were baptized again, there is no evidence of such with Apollos. He had been baptized with some limitations in his theology, but he was clearly a believer who had fulfilled the essential components of the Gospel, namely faith and repentance as outlined in Acts 20:21, making a second baptism unnecessary.

The Holy Spirit came upon them in Acts 19:6 as Paul laid his hands upon them after their baptism in water. Speaking in tongues and prophesying were evident, but there is no interpretation as is mentioned in 1 Corinthians. A similar order of events took place among the Samaritans in Acts 8:14–17, but there was no mention of tongues or prophecy in that passage.

There is yet another variation of this among the Gentiles in Caesarea in Acts 10:44–48. While Peter was preaching, he and the other Jewish believers witnessed the coming of the Holy Spirit upon the gathered Gentiles. There was no laying on of hands, but there was the manifestation of tongues. In this scenario, water baptism was administered after the Holy Spirit had done His work.

This all reminds us of John 3:14, where Jesus explained the sovereign movements of the Holy Spirit: He cannot be boxed into our neatly packaged theological systems, nor can He be utilized or controlled for our own selfish interests, as Simon found out in Acts 8:18–24.

*The Henry Morris Study Bible* makes the observation that this is the only instance in the New Testament where anyone is rebaptized. The obvious question this raises is how these disciples differ from Apollos, who didn't have to be baptized a second time. You be the judge, but it seems to me that the answer raises even more questions about this difficult passage:

> Presumably the difference was that the Ephesian disciples had been baptized by one or more of John's disciples, after the coming of the Holy Spirit at Pentecost when Christ's disciples first began to "baptize" in the name of Jesus Christ (2:38).[168]

[168] Morris, *The Henry Morris Study Bible*, 1676.

The real question that needs to be addressed is simply this: accepting that these disciples were truly born again, why were they required to submit to a second water baptism? The Morris notes suggest that the knowledge they had was sufficient for salvation but in some way deficient enough to require a rebaptism.[169] In what way was it deficient? Does this in some way cheapen the quality of John's baptism?

James White insists in quite dynamic terms that the preposition *since* should be changed to *when* in Acts 19:2, suggesting that the King James Version translators made a major error here and opened the passage up to some dangerous implications regarding a secondary work of the Holy Spirit in the life of the believer. He still doesn't tell us why these twelve men had to be baptized again. Rather than answering the obvious questions arising from the text, White's only motivation is to put a negative spin on the integrity of the King James Version translators.[170]

Those translators have, in this instance, been unfairly treated. The Geneva translators (1560–1599) used the same word as the King James Version translation team (*"since ye believed"*) while Tyndale's New Testament reads *"after ye believed."* The Strong's Concordance offers a number of alternative readings, including *since* and *after*, but the word *when* is absent from the discussion, which in itself is interesting.

I am convinced that these twelve men were certainly lacking, but to a far greater degree than has so far been suggested. They were in the same category as those found in Matthew 7:21–27. They were not Christians.

We do not ask professing Christians to enter the waters of baptism a second time because they lack knowledge, which seems to be the strawman offered by commentators on this

[169] Ibid., 1675.

[170] White, *The King James Only Controversy*, 285–286.

passage. These men were asked to be baptized only after they had demonstrated that their so-called earlier baptism had been entered into without possession of saving faith.

In his comments on the spiritual state of Judas Iscariot, Marvin Fieldhouse tells us how close we can be and yet so far from the kingdom:

> Let every man take warning who has any lust in his life which he is thinking to satiate at the expense of righteousness. Judas teaches us that a man [or woman] can be near Jesus, follow Him, hear Him and use Him without loving Him![171]

John MacArthur raises the bar even higher: "Not everyone who calls himself a Christian really is. Unbelievers do make false professions of faith in Christ, and people who are not truly Christians can be deceived into thinking they are believers."[172]

For those who teach that Acts 19 is the formula for receiving the Holy Spirit, and that it must be accompanied by tongues, etc., they must explain why the formula obviously failed in Acts 8:14–17, since in that case there was no tongues and no prophecy.

In my estimation, the only view that truly satisfies Acts 19:1–7 is that which sees twelve religious yet unsaved men being led to Christ, then being baptized by the Apostle Paul. Further to this, they had received the fullness of the Holy Spirit, accompanied by tongues and prophesying *after* they were baptized.

The Book of Acts is transitional and hardly matches the kind of order developed in the later epistles of Paul. The

---

171 Marvin Fieldhouse, *Missionary's Bible Commentary, Volume 3: 84 Lessons* (Nagano, Japan: Oriental Bible Study Fellowship), 614.

172 John MacArthur, *The Gospel According to Jesus* (Grand Rapids, MI: Academic Books, 1988), 37.

experience of these men is not unlike a number of others in Acts that signals the availability of the Holy Spirit to all, both Jews and Gentiles.

The usual order witnessed now, according to Romans 8:9, is salvation by faith accompanied by the indwelling of the Holy Spirit, after which the convert enters, or should enter, the waters of baptism, with the acceptable mode being immersion (although some differ here). With all due respect to believers from a variety of backgrounds, I fail to see any biblical support for infant baptism. Even should we accept, as some do (I do not), that tongues should be experienced by every believer as part of a special filling of the Spirit following conversion, this surely cannot be more important than salvation itself and should not be made such.

The situation that arose in Acts 19:1–7 must be seen against the background of the ministry of John the Baptist. Some dispensationalists have relegated the son of Zacharias and Elisabeth (Luke 1:12–13) to a rather obscure Old Testament ministry that did little more than predict the coming of the Messiah. This is hardly the stance of Scripture. John's ministry was pivotal and of prime importance.

According to Matthew 11:11–12 and Luke 16:16, John is seen as a preacher of the kingdom of heaven which is already in existence. He is a full contradiction to our predetermined theological systems being filled with the Holy Spirit in his mother's womb, reminding us of Jeremiah, who was sanctified and ordained for ministry while yet unborn (Jeremiah 1:5).

John Broadus is careful to remind us,

> The inference is often drawn that he (John) belonged entirely to the Old Testament dispensation. It is frequently asserted and by many taken for granted, that the kingdom of heaven began on the Day of Pentecost,

> following our Lord's ascension, and so John had no connection with it except to predict its approach.[173]

This raises the question of what age John belonged to. Notice the word *until* in Matthew 11:13. He belongs to this dispensation and he inaugurated it with his preaching. Also notice the connection made by Peter in Acts 1:22 and Acts 10:37.

Dr. W.A. Criswell stated, "The Christian movement began with John."[174] S.E. Anderson makes the assertion, "Since John's ministry *overlapped* that of Christ and the apostles (John 4:1,2), then we can be sure they were similar and in the same dispensation."[175]

Anderson has done a great deal to remind us of the importance of John's ministry to kingdom truth. He preached repentance and pointed the people to their Messiah. His baptism was authenticated by the Lord Jesus Himself. His converts included at least some of the twelve apostles (John 1:35–45). He baptized them and their baptism was seen as legitimate. They had no need to repeat their baptism at a later time.

John also preached about the Holy Spirit, which should be enough to convince us that the twelve men in Acts 19:1–7 were never baptized by John himself, as they told Paul they knew nothing about the Holy Spirit.

Anderson makes the observation that some dispensationalists, including the Plymouth Brethren have made "too much division between Jews and the Gentiles in the New Testament; they spilt the New Testament into compartments… they downgrade him into the Old Testament."[176] It is time to bring John the Baptist into the New Testament where he rightly belongs.

---

[173] Anderson, *Baptists Unshackled*, 19.

[174] Ibid., 22.

[175] Ibid.

[176] Ibid., 112.

## PAUL'S EXIT FROM EPHESUS

Toward the end of Paul's ministry in Ephesus, the silversmith guild, led by a man called Demetrius, incited such violent riots in the streets that Paul was forced to make a hasty exit after some parting words of encouragement to his followers (Acts 20:1). The centrepiece of Ephesian idolatry was the goddess Diana, which was essentially fashioned after a meteorite that had fallen on the city many years before and was housed in a heathen temple. The silversmiths had made miniature shrines of the temple and sold them at exorbitant prices to the populace but then became alarmed at Paul's preaching, fearful that the people would abandon Diana, thus cutting into their lucrative business. Calm was restored to the city after intervention by the chief magistrates.

Anticipating that his ministry to Ephesus was coming to a close, and prior to the uproar in the streets, Paul's strategy for future mission endeavours is laid out in Acts 19:21, which provides an outline for the remainder of Acts. Paul intended to visit Jerusalem after visiting churches in Macedonia and Achaia, which included churches in Philippi, Thessalonica, Berea, and Corinth. From Jerusalem, his goal was to reach the imperial city of Rome, which would then provide a stepping stone to Spain (Romans 15:24–28).

Once Ephesus became calm, Paul met with the Christians to encourage them and then left for Macedonia (Acts 20:1).

A careful reading of the early verses of Acts 20 shows us that Luke rejoined Paul's missionary entourage at Philippi and travelled together with them to Troas. It was here that a young teenager by the name of Eutychus fell asleep during one of Paul's sermons, then fell to his death from a third-floor window (Acts 20: 9). After this, Paul restored him to life (Acts 20:9).

Paul was once again in a hurry to get to Jerusalem (Acts 18:22), with the hope of being there on the day of Pentecost (Acts 20:16).

Once Paul arrived in Mitylene, chief city of the Isle of Lesbos and located thirty miles south of Ephesus, he requested that the church elders meet him there for a farewell gathering. Luke gives us the details of this very touching and emotional time of fellowship. It ended with much prayer and weeping before Paul was accompanied to his ship by the grateful Ephesians who would never see Paul again this side of heaven (Acts 20:17–38).

Since the very early days of the church, there have been those who question Paul's decision to go to Jerusalem, with much of their argument coming from the account given in Acts 21:1–14. As Paul made his way to Jerusalem, his stops in Tyre and Caesarea were met with repeated warnings not to place Jerusalem on his itinerary. These objections are difficult to refute, as is evidenced by the Scriptures themselves (Acts 21:4, 11). Some will argue strongly that Paul's insistence on going to Jerusalem was more of a personal obsession rather than the leading of the Holy Spirit. As we see from the scriptures just given, caution not to proceed to the Jewish centre of worship came from individuals who themselves claimed to be led of God. It does seem, however, that Paul was indeed led of God in his desire and wouldn't be dissuaded by any prospect of coming hardship (Acts 19:21, 20:22–24, 21:13–14).

Paul's third missionary journey came to an end with his arrival in Jerusalem where he was warmly received by the church leaders and reported to them what God had been doing among the Gentiles (Acts 21:14–19).

At this time in the early church, there were major adjustments and sometimes irritating misunderstandings as converted Jews and Gentiles were brought into the church and began to worship and work together as one. The Jerusalem council in Acts 15 tried their best to appease both sides, but it became increasingly difficult to reach the Jewish population who felt that Paul and his followers spent most of their time criticizing the Jewish religious system.

In an effort to address this chasm, Paul went into the temple to embrace a Jewish rite of purification so as not to lose his Jewish identity among his own people. While there, some Jews from Asia, probably from Ephesus, entered the temple and accused him of taking a Gentile into a forbidden area of the temple complex, possibly in reference to his previous visit (Acts 18:19–22). Paul was then dragged outside the temple and being severely beaten (Acts 21:32).

From Acts 21:33–22:22, Paul was arrested and taken into custody by the Roman authorities, but with permission from the Roman commander he gave a stirring address to the Jewish people in which he shared his conversion on the road to Damascus. His defence was heard—until he shared God's call to witness to the Gentiles, at which time the unruly crowd asked the authorities to take him away from their presence. The opposition to Paul was so strong that the Roman commander decided to put Paul under torture in order to extract information and determine why the Jews found him so offensive. Facing severe suffering, or even death, Paul appealed to his Roman citizenship for protection.

Little is known of Paul prior to his appearance in Acts except from his own writings in the Scriptures and a few other isolated accounts in ancient literature. We know that Paul came from Tarsus in Asia Minor, or modern-day Turkey. Cilicia, of which Tarsus was a part, became a Roman province under Pompey in 65 BC. Located on a busy trade route, it was a centre of industry and intellectualism only thirty miles south of the famous Cilician Gates, a well-travelled pass through which many ancient armies travelled. Some sources indicate that Paul's parents were Jews from the area of Galilee and for unknown reasons moved to Tarsus where they took out Roman citizenship. This is where Paul was born, but there is little agreement as to when he left his home city and moved to Jerusalem, where he studied Old Testament laws and customs under the famous teacher and philosopher Gamaliel (Acts 5:34, 22:3).[177]

Fearing discipline from his superiors for ill-treatment of a Roman citizen, the Roman commander detained Paul overnight and the next

[177] Herbert Lockyer, *All the Apostles of the Bible* (Grand Rapids, MI: Zondervan, 1974), 206–209.

morning ordered the Jewish council and the chief priests to be brought together so they could hear Paul's defence.

In Acts 23:1–10, Paul faced a mixed crowd of Pharisees and Sadducees, none of them friendly. Fearful that Paul would be killed by the unruly mob, the commander had Paul confined to the barracks for his protection. In Acts 23:11, Paul received assurance from the Lord that he would be kept safe in Jerusalem, and in time he would witness for his Lord in Rome.

## A FOILED PLOT

Seething with anger, more than forty men hatched a plot to kill Paul in Acts 23:12–22, but their plan fell apart when Paul's nephew was able to enter the barracks and warn his uncle of impending danger. This tells us that Paul's extended family members in Jerusalem were well known and respected by the authorities. This information was then passed on to the commander, who made an immediate decision to send Paul to Caesarea, the Roman capital of Palestine, under armed escort.

Luke clearly had firsthand information about these events, as is evidenced by his detailed account of the letter that accompanied the centurions to Caesarea (Acts 23:26–30). From Luke's account, we learn the name of the commander at the barracks in Jerusalem, Claudius Lysias. The letter was addressed to Felix, a former slave and the Roman governor of Judea, a position he held from AD 52–59.

## THE THREE SISTERS

We learn from Acts 23:31 that Paul and his protectors spent the first night at Antipatris, a common stopover that was named for Antipater, the Jewish father of Herod the Great.

As we enter Acts 24, Felix has invited the Jewish council to come to Caesarea and state their case against Paul at a court hearing. The

Jewish delegation including the high priest Ananias and a lawyer called Tertullus arrived five days later to lay charges against Paul. Following some legal wrangling between Paul and his accusers, Felix ended the proceedings by by saying he would deal with it later.

Paul was kept in custody with limited freedoms but was often invited to meet with Felix and his wife Drusilla to discuss what was then known as "the Way" (Acts 24:22), or the Christian faith. There is no evidence that either of them was ever converted.

Drusilla and her sisters Mariamne (not named in Scripture) and Bernice were granddaughters of Herod the Great (Matthew 2:16), which means they were of Jewish descent through their great-grandfather, Antipater. These sisters were also the daughters of Herod Agrippa I, with Drusilla being the youngest and according to descriptions of the time the most beautiful of the trio. We have already written of their father who died in great agony (Acts 12:20–23); his horrible death is also recorded in the writings of the historian Josephus.

A further note of interest is that these sisters were also the nieces of Herod Antipas, who was responsible for the death of John the Baptist.[178]

Felix confined Paul for two years and had hoped to receive a financial bribe for his release (Acts 24:26). Wanting to curry the favour of the Jews, he left Paul in prison even after he was released from his duties in AD 59. From there, he disappears into history.[179]

Josephus provides an added footnote about Drusilla. In AD 79, Mount Vesuvius exploded in a molten sea of lava, burying everything in its pathway including the cities of Pompeii and Herculaneum. Included among the victims who waited too long to escape from the fiery inferno were Drusilla and her son Agrippa.[180]

The successor to Felix was not only an efficient leader but a shrewd operator. From the outset, Festus determined to bring about a quick

---

[178] Whiston, ed., *The Works of Josephus*, 412–413.

[179] Brand, ed., *The Holman Illustrated Bible Dictionary*, 444.

[180] Lockyer, *The Women of the Bible*, 49.

resolution to the situation with Paul and went almost immediately to Jerusalem to confer with the Jewish leaders. Insisting that all proceedings take place in Caesarea, he returned home to await the arrival of the Jewish delegation. Paul's second hearing was no long, drawn-out affair. With the Jews unable to find an accusation against Paul that had substance, and with Paul claiming innocence of any wrongdoing, Festus went to his advisors and in one fell swoop had the entire affair turned over to the emperor in Rome (Acts 25:12).

If Paul had any illusions about having his case heard before Nero in the near future, he was sadly mistaken. Luke tells of two visitors coming to pay Festus an extended visit and pay their respects to the new Judean governor. Their names were Herod Agrippa II and Bernice (Acts 25:13).

Herod Agrippa II, the last of the Herods of any prominence in the New Testament, was the son of Herod Agrippa I, whose life and death were recorded in Acts 12. This is the Herod who had James, the brother of John, put to death and imprisoned Peter to please the Jews; he probably had plans to have Peter executed. This is also the same Herod mentioned in regard to the infamous three sisters who died in terrible agony (Acts 12:20–23).

Bernice and Agrippa were brother and sister, living as man and wife. Their incestuous relationship was the stuff of gossip in Rome where Agrippa had been raised. At the time of his visit to Festus in Caesarea, he was in charge of the kingdom of Chalcis, located northwest of Damascus in Syria. His position gave him the right to appoint the high priest at the temple in Jerusalem.

After being twice widowed, her second marriage being to her own uncle, Bernice moved in with her brother Agrippa. Acting as his consort, she was often presented as his queen. She later left her brother and married Ptolemy, King of Cilicia, but soon deserted him and returned to her brother. Her escapades were far from over, however, as she eventually made her way to Rome where she became mistress to Emperor Vespasian. Leaving Vespasian, she then became mistress to his son Titus, the Roman general who conquered Jerusalem in AD 70. When Titus became emperor following his father's death in AD 79, he banished Bernice from his home and she subsequently returned to her brother.[181]

The visit of Agrippa and Bernice to Caesarea soon triggered another hearing for Paul. While Felix often asked Paul to leave his presence out of extreme fear (Acts 24:25), Festus acted indifferently and saw the dispute between Paul and the Jews in Jerusalem as simple disagreements about a man called Jesus. Festus wasn't familiar with the finer points of Judaism, which is probably why he engaged Agrippa and Bernice in conversation, knowing they were more proficient about Jewish laws and could better relate to the situation with his prisoner.

With his curiosity greatly aroused, Agrippa requested an audience with Paul. This third hearing had no lawyer present, no delegation from Jerusalem, and no decision-making powers but, it provided Paul with a platform to give a much more detailed description of the Gospel than either of the other two hearings.

From Acts 25:23–27, we learn that Festus was at a loss as to what to do with Paul, which charges to lay against him, if any, and what information he should pass on to Nero in his report. Prominent leaders of the city, along with military personnel, attended along with Agrippa, Bernice, and of course Paul.

It is with this setting in mind that we enter into Acts 26:1–32, which encompasses Paul's final hearing before leaving for Rome. Since Paul wasn't on trial, and none of his accusers were present, the conversation in this chapter is lively and relaxed. Paul again shared his conversion experience on the road to Damascus and knew he had a captive audience in Agrippa and Bernice, who were Jewish and anxious to know what Paul had to say. An interesting outburst came from Festus as he accused Paul of allowing his intellectual skills to drive him to near insanity, to which Paul gave an instant rebuttal (Acts 26:24–25).

Toward the end of the chapter, and at the end of the hearing Agrippa, Festus, and Bernice stood to their feet and drew aside for a

---

[181] *Liberty Bible Commentary*, 2193.

brief tête-a-tête during which they determine that Paul was innocent and had he not appealed to Caesar could have been released on the spot (Acts 26:30–32).

The exchange between Paul and Agrippa in Acts 26:27–29 has prompted endless conversation among Christians as to whether Agrippa was under real conviction. Many argue that Agrippa interrupted Paul to remind him that his argument presumed too much about persuading him to become a Christian and that he was far from convinced. In other words, he was literally making fun of Paul and using the moment to impress his unbelieving consort, Bernice. Others argue that Agrippa was under deep conviction, which prompted him to bring an end to the hearing.

## PAUL'S ARRIVAL IN ROME

The last two chapters of Acts tell of Paul's journey to Rome. Some wouldn't consider this a fourth missionary journey because Paul was going to Italy as a prisoner, which was certainly not in his original scheme, but he does reach his destination.

From the use again of the "we" and "us" pronouns, we know that Luke had rejoined Paul. Just exactly how a physician was able to board a voyage to Italy on a boat full of prisoners (Acts 28:1), we are not told. We can only conjecture.

In order to get the most from your reading of these last two chapters of Acts, it is imperative to access a good map that shows Paul's voyage from Caesarea to Rome. It is also advised to consult a good Bible dictionary to study the background of some of the names and places that are mentioned. Some of the names have not changed since ancient times.

Luke is very exacting in his facts and figures, showing the manifest of the ship as well as the number of passengers and crew on board, which he reveals as 276 (Acts 27:37). He even gives us the names of some of the crew. This number no doubt includes the extra crewmembers who were part of the second ship they had boarded at Myra, located at the southern tip of modern-day Turkey.

Almost from the first day, the voyage was plagued by severe winds (Acts 27:4) that constantly played havoc with the ship's crew and passengers. Following a stop in Sidon, where Paul was able to meet with friends and receive provisions, they proceeded around the Isle of Cyprus to the north and continued west to Myra where all were transferred to another ship. Located north of Alexandria, Egypt, this would have been the ideal stopping place for a ship sailing to Italy.

The Alexandrian ship in Acts 27:6 would have been part of the imperial fleet that carried Egyptian grain to Italy. The next verse indicates that trouble continued to follow these voyagers even after transferring to another vessel. Finding themselves within sight of Cnidus meant they were already off-course, since they would have ordinarily sailed south of Rhodes and north of Crete en route to Italy. They did manage to stay close to Crete on the southern side, but due to hesitations and disputes on board they failed to make a landing where they could winter.

When the ship was hit by a vicious northeaster called Euroclydon, they found themselves tossed about in the open seas with little hope of survival. Gear and grain were thrown overboard in an effort to lighten the vessel. Paul remained calm throughout since he had already been assured by God that all would be kept safe, and he knew that God had destined him to minister in Rome.

The reference to Adria in Acts 27:27 has puzzled some, since Paul and his fellow prisoners were being pitched about in almost total darkness in the Great Sea, the Mediterranean. How could Adria, now the Adriatic, be found in the middle of the Mediterranean? The Greek text on which our English translations are based is fully accurate. The present-day Adriatic Sea was then called the Gulf of Adria, which at that time extended much farther south than it does today, which would position Paul's ship at the southern tip of this gulf.[182]

As the ship ran aground on the present day Isle of Malta, it broke up and it was every man for himself. But all got ashore safely and not a single person was lost (Acts 27:43–44). After spending three months

[182] *ESV Study Bible*, 2143. See notation Acts 27:27.

on this island, Paul and company boarded another Alexandrian ship and sailed for Italy (Acts 28:11–14).

Particulars about Paul's time in Rome are wanting, but we do know from Luke's closing chapter that Paul was placed under house arrest for two years and was free to receive his friends. He witnessed freely to the Jews of Rome and saw many of them come to faith in Christ.

Based on Romans 15:24–28, we know that Paul had it in mind to extend his ministry to Spain, but the question is whether he got there. Drawing from hints in the pastoral epistles, as well as certain writings that have come down to us from the second century, some researchers are convinced that Paul was released in AD 63, after which he visited Spain as well as the Aegean region. He was probably rearrested in AD 67 on orders from Nero, who at that time had turned on Christians with a vengeance. Tradition persists that later that same year, Paul was led by his captors out to the Appian Way (some say the Ostian Way) where he was beheaded by a Roman executioner.

If we count Hebrews, Paul's writings represent a full fourteen books of the New Testament.

Luke brings the Book of Acts to an abrupt end with reference to Paul's continuing ministry from his rented house in Rome. Acts 28:12 references Paul's ongoing emphasis on the Kingdom of God, as well as his boldness in proclaiming the Gospel of Christ until his voice was silenced by an executioner.

This brings an end to Luke's sequel to the Gospel he had written earlier, making him the only one of the four Gospel writers to leave us a follow-up. Luke's sequel is one "we should be eternally grateful for, since without it the knowledge of the early Christians would be greatly diminished."[183] In terms of sheer volume, Luke has left us two volumes that represent more material than the total writings of the Apostle Paul.

---

[183] J. Stephen Lang, *Know the Bible in 30 Days* (Tulsa, OK: Woohoo! Inc., 2008), 381–382.

## THE KINGDOM NOW MOVEMENT**

Known as Kingdom Now, or "dominion theology," this influential segment of Christianity emanated from Pentecostalism but has been rejected as being radical and unscriptural by many, but not all Pentecostals. This strange religious concoction has spread its tentacles into a number of denominations as well as those of the Pentecostal persuasion.

In one of their signature books, *The Age of the Saints*, author Bill Hamon encourages his adherents to infiltrate existing churches with the express purpose of bringing them online with the "healing of the land" genre. He further encourages his followers to vacate those churches that resist the Kingdom Now agenda and urges them to open up new ministries that promote the Kingdom Now persuasion.[184]

Besides Hamon, this movement is also championed by such notables as Cindy Jacobs and C. Peter Wagner. Some of their major tenets include the following:

- Apostles and prophets are now being restored to the church with the ability to heal the sick and raise the dead.[185] People who are truly healed will stay healed.[186] The age of miracles experienced in the early days of the church will be far exceeded by the apostles and prophets of today.[187]
- Luke 19:10 has nothing to do with lost souls in hell but refers instead to the original dominion over creation

[184] Dr. Bill Hamon, *The Day of the Saints* (Shippensburg, PA, Destiny Image, 2002), 197–198.

[185] Ibid., 107, 175–178, 323–324.

[186] Ibid., 273–275.

[187] Ibid., 36–38.

forfeited by Adam in the garden of Eden that will be restored in our time. Little discussion is given to a deteriorating culture and a church under trial and duress (2 Timothy 3:1–13).[188]

- Major emphasis is placed on tongues, healings, and miracles.[189]
- People can be transported from place to place much like Philip in Acts 8:39.[190]
- The Lord Jesus Christ shares His office as Mediator with us (1 Timothy 2:5 and Hebrews 7:25). How did one become more than one?[191]

This entire movement is essentially a throwback to the Latter Rain movement of the 1950s, which is recognized by Bill Hamon. This earlier version of the more modern equipping-of-the-saints ministry left the scene early, resulting in some churches in shambles.

With no scriptural warrant, Hamon pegs the final push for restoration in 2030. Surely, right-thinking Christians need to beware of this kind of off-the-wall theology that speaks of Christians being activated to bringing God's kingdom to the world, with a manmade timeline as well.[192]

God has not called His people to bring about permanent change in a culture that is under His judgment. He has not called us to bring a message of permanent healing to the sick. We are not set aside to be trained in zeal and the supernatural, as is

---

188 C. Peter Wagner, *Dominion! How Kingdom Action Can Change the World* (Grand Rapids, MI: Chosen, 2008), 69–70.

189 Hamon, *The Day of the Saints*, 159–162, 306.

190 Ibid., 96.

191 Cindy Jacobs, *Possessing the Gates of the Enemy* (Grand Rapids, MI: Chosen, 2009), 60–61.

192 Hamon, *The Day of the Saints*, 134, 164–168.

claimed by Bill Hamon.[193] Some of this lends itself to the bizarre and the ridiculous. We are not called to effect the resurrection of the dead. That is God's department, not ours. Well has one writer said, "People need to avoid extreme teachings that bring them into bondage. If a teaching seems weird or unbalanced, it probably is."[194]

According to Hamon, unscrupulous persons can operate in the gifting of the Spirit; moral character and/or theological integrity are not required for them to minister.[195] The wealth of the world is to be transferred to the church.[196] Hamon freely admits that the Latter Rain movement made some major mistakes, including the making of false promises. He claims that the present Day of the Saints movement will avoid these past miscues.[197]

C. Peter Wagner states that the Azusa Street revival of 1906 began to bring the work of the Holy Spirit into its proper place.[198] He further suggests that signs and wonders will become normal for all Christians, with the original apostles being outdistanced by the present movement.[199] Wagner claims that the body of Christ is now represented by Charismatic evangelicals.[200]

The Pentecostals who resist the ministries of apostles and prophets are especially singled out for chastisement by Bill Hamon.[201] He compares himself to Habakkuk in the

---

[193] Ibid., 188.

[194] Ralph Woodrow, *A Balanced Christian Discerns Extremes* (Palm Springs, CA: Ralph Woodrow Evangelistic Association, 2005), 31.

[195] Hamon, *The Day of the Saints*, 317–318.

[196] Ibid., 278–279.

[197] Ibid., 140, 319.

[198] Wagner, *Dominion!*, 25.

[199] Ibid., 111–112.

[200] Hamon, *The Day of the Saints*, 188–189.

[201] Ibid.

Old Testament as he lays out his vision for the church of the future.[202] Wagner acknowledges that this movement is rejected by the Assemblies of God.[203] The Kingdom Now movement places a primary emphasis on a cultural mandate to improve society rather than the work of soul-winning.[204]

Tom Stipe is a former member of the board of directors for the Association of Vineyard Churches. During a leadership conference in the midwestern United States some years ago, Stipe told the attendants,

> The prophets began to inform us that in the last days, the Lord was restoring the fivefold ministry of apostles, prophets, pastors, teachers, and evangelists to the church. We were challenged to accept the arrival of apostles and prophets because today's church already had plenty of teaching, pastoring, and evangeling. The arrival of the prophets and apostles would lead to the world's last and greatest revival.[205]

Stipe, as a pastor and author, bought into the movement and led his church into the adoption of Kingdom Now policies and teachings. It was a decision he would live to regret. Over a period of time, his church began losing members and losing interest in the Bible. Signs, wonders, and prophecies replaced the teachings of the Word of God.

He later resigned from the Vineyard Association and brought his church back to a more balanced and biblical position. He found the emphasis of Kingdom Now to be sorely lacking in scriptural support, and his own life went through a dry spell as a direct result of this so-called prophetical ministry. When he

[202] Ibid., 119–120.

[203] Wagner, *Dominion!*, 62.

[204] Hamon, *The Day of the Saints*, 250–252.

[205] Hanegraaff, *Counterfeit Revival*, x.

took his church back to the basic teachings of the Bible, God began to bless it in singular fashion.

Stipe's experience is a lesson for all of us who may be tempted to adopt an emphasis that may sound good but clearly lacks the support of Scripture. From one account, Stipe gives us these words, which he had learned early in his ministry from one of his mentors: "When you're not sure what God is saying, go back to what God has already said."[206] Excellent advice!

This dubious sect is distinctively mystical in nature and is frontloaded with often extreme emotionalism combined with excessive repetition. My personal assessment is that this movement represents an unbridled enthusiasm for an unbalanced and unbiblical emphasis. Discerning Christians will search the Scriptures to ascertain whether these things are so (Acts 17:11).

[206] Ibid., xii–xvi.

# The Epistle of Paul to the Romans

The author of this epistle is the Apostle Paul. There is almost full agreement that Paul wrote this letter to the Christians in Rome from the city of Corinth while on his third missionary journey (Acts 20:1–3).

There are sixteen chapters in the book of Romans broken into:

- The Introduction (1:1–7)
- Paul's Desire to Come to Rome (1:8–15)
- The Essence of the Gospel (1:16–17)
- Depravity Defined (1:18–32)
- God Is Impartial (2:1–29)
- The Entire World Is Guilty (3:1–20)
- Justification by Faith (3:21–5:21)
- Dead to Sin (6:1–23)
- The Connection (7:1–13)
- The Conflict (7:14–25)
- Deliverance and Victory (8:1–39)
- The Sovereignty of God (9:1–33)

- Faith and Salvation (10:1–21)
- The Remnant of Israel (11:1–36)
- Dedicated for Service (12:1–21)
- Civil Authority (13:1–14)
- Conscience (14:1–23)
- Self-Denial (15:1–13)
- Priority of the Gospel (15:14–33)
- Expressions of Love (16:1–22)

## SUMMARY

"And the Grandeur that was Rome."[207]—Edgar Allen Poe

The cultural melting pot that existed in Italy three thousand years ago, and which ultimately converged on a site consisting of seven hills where the Latin plain found its way to the Tiber River, has a checkered history that is at once complicated, confusing, and controversial. The confluence of tradition, legend, myth, and reality has made it a herculean task to sort out fact from fiction.

The Roman and Greek writers only compounded the problem by imposing their own fables and fantasies on an already convoluted historical account.

The city of seven hills we now know as Rome has been given the traditional founding date of 753 BC. Long after this date, legends began to swirl about twin boys by the names of Romulus and Remus, who after being abandoned on the banks of the Tiber were adopted, suckled, and raised by a she-wolf. Later on, by ingenuity and intrigue, Romulus founded the city of Rome.[208]

---

[207] Edgar Allen Poe, *Great Tales and Poems* (Toronto, CA: Vintage Books, 2009), 15.

[208] Cary and Scullard, *A History of Rome*, 35, 39–40.

## THE ROAD TO EMPIRE

Though details are lacking, history concedes that for more than two hundred years Rome and its surrounding area was ruled by a number of successive kings. All of this changed in 510 BC with an obvious power struggle that saw the regal line abruptly dismissed, to be replaced with a dual governorship in concert with a powerful Senate.

A story still embedded in Italian folklore may have some tiny shreds of truth. It indicates that a moral and political scandal may have ended the kingship, and from that time forward no ruler in Rome was to use the title of king. The story goes that a man called Sextus, son of the king, raped Lucretia, wife of a noble. The rapist was later tracked down and killed, while his father and two brothers were forced to flee the city. The monarchy was then abolished to be replaced by two annually elected consuls, or governors.[209]

Over the next century, Rome was forced to flex its military muscle on numerous occasions as surrounding people groups harassed the newly founded republic.

In 405 BC, the fortunes of Rome changed dramatically when this growing city-state launched a major campaign against the stronghold of Veii, located just northwest of the city, which represented an ongoing threat to the security of the republic. Nearly ten years later, in 396 BC, the Romans made their final assault on this almost impregnable city situated at the top of a mountainous rock. Using the techniques of siege warfare, they captured the fortress, massacred many of its townsfolk, and sold the survivors into slavery.

Historians now know what even the Romans didn't know then: this was the first step in Rome's quest for world domination. Less than a thousand years after its founding, Rome was destined to become the centre of the mightiest empire the world had ever witnessed, spreading its tentacles well beyond the Italian promontory into Great Britain, France, Persia, the Aegean, the Mediterranean, Palestine, Spain, and

[209] Ibid., 55.

Arabia. Some analysts suggest that, at its peak, the Roman Empire embraced no less than twenty-five percent of the globe.[210]

## CAESAR AUGUSTUS

When Julius Caesar crossed the Rubicon in 49 BC, he changed the course of the empire as well as world history. Ignoring advice from the Senate, he refused to disband his army and marched into Rome a virtual dictator. Some would suggest he was the first real emperor of Rome.

Upon his assassination in 44 BC, there followed fifteen years of civil war and political unrest. In 29 BC, Caesar's nephew and adopted son Octavian became the undisputed ruler of the Roman Empire, receiving full support from the Senate in Rome. Distancing himself from the hated kingly rule that had precipitated republican government in 510 BC., as well as the violence and bloodshed that had characterized his rise to power, he changed his name to Caesar Augustus, becoming the first fully recognized emperor of Rome. His rule of over forty years ended with his death in AD 14. He is named in Luke 2:1 as being leader of the Roman Empire when Christ was born in Bethlehem.[211]

The passing of Augustus unleashed a fifty-year family dynasty with the next four emperors related by blood to either the first emperor or his third wife, Livia.

The second emperor, Tiberius, son of Augustus, ruled from AD 14–37 and is named in the Scriptures (Luke 3:1). The tyrannical emperor Caligula was assassinated in AD 41 after four years of inept rule. Next in line was Claudius, who in spite of being handicapped by a congenital defect ruled for thirteen years.

Of interest to Bible students is that on orders of Claudius many Jews were forced to leave Rome in AD 49, including Aquila and

---

210 Ibid., 71–75.

211 Smith, Muzzey, and Lloyd, *World History* (Toronto, ON: Ginn and Company), 87–89.

Priscilla, who met up with the Apostle Paul in the city of Corinth (Acts 18:2). Very possibly this was when Paul's interest in a trip to Rome was initiated. Little did he know that he would arrive there years later under an armed guard after a harrowing sea voyage that began in Caesarea (Acts 27–28).

The last emperor of this family line was Nero, whose rule lasted from AD 54–68. Nero's early years were marked by a distinct toleration of Christianity, but the later years saw him turn on Christians with hatred and viciousness. He probably spoke to Paul face to face, but having little patience with religious dissidents at this time in his rule he gave the order to have Paul executed, probably a year before his own death in AD 68.[212]

## THE CHURCH AT ROME

The Rome of Paul's day had become a centre of the arts. Drawing from financial resources in three continents, this city on the Tiber River was a playground for the rich oozing with every kind of pleasure imaginable. One observer has stated that Rome was "a place that provided every virtue and vice known to mankind."[213] Rome's engineering expertise including paved roads and drainage systems, some of which are still in use, a testament to the vitality of the civilization the Romans brought to every country which they entered and conquered.

Renowned for their reputation of raising large armies and absorbing the strength of their foes, often making them allies of their massive empire, the Romans were superior to any other military force they would face.

The Jewish presence in Rome was substantial, as is evidenced by the inscriptions on remains from the first century that can still be examined. The expulsion of AD 49 affected only a limited number of Jews, doing little to blunt their influence.

---

[212] Cary and Scullard, *A History of Rome*, 351–358.

[213] *ESV Study Bible*, 2154.

As Paul wrote to the Romans, there is some debate as to how strong the church was at that time. Some are convinced that relations between the Jews and the church, comprised of both Jews and Gentiles, were strained at the time of Paul's writing, while others feel that relations were relatively calm. One thing is certain: Paul's letter to the Romans is a theological and literary masterpiece that represents the very heart of the Gospel for both Jews and Gentiles.[214]

Writers of church history are more than a little divided as to when the church of Rome was founded and by whom. Possibly Jewish Christians came to Rome following the day of Pentecost, while some may have fled there on the heels of the persecution that came in the wake of the death of Stephen. They would have witnessed to their kinsmen already living in Rome as well as to their Gentile acquaintances.

Some would argue that the church of Rome was founded by Peter, especially our Roman Catholic friends, but there is little evidence that such is the case. What we know for certain is that at the time of Paul's epistle there was a strong Christian presence in the "eternal city," and the apostle addresses issues that apply to both Jews and Gentiles.

Bible students looking for details of local church organization and polity will fail to find such in Paul's letter to the Romans. Lovers of prophecy who try to fathom the depths of predictive Scripture or find a detailed summary of last-day events will come up empty. Paul's major thrust in Romans is to explore in depth what the Gospel is and what it isn't.[215]

Of interest to historians is that in the writings of Suetonius, a Roman biographer and antiquarian, there is a reference to one Chrestos (Christ) whose teachings had sparked an ongoing controversy among the Jews of Rome and resulted in the expulsion of a part of the Jewish population in AD 49.[216] This means that for a time Gentiles

---

[214] Douglas I. Moo, *Encountering the Book of Romans* (Grand Rapids, MI: Baker Academic, 2002), 27.

[215] Ibid., 35.

[216] Ibid., 27–211.

outnumbered their Jewish counterparts in the church of Rome, with a resultant tension that Paul would be made well aware of by his contact with Aquila and Priscilla.

Paul's extensive treatment of the Gospel in Romans is designed to address all Jewish-Gentile issues and to show them as one redeemed body in Christ. The first line of the argument, which introduces the book of Romans in the 1560 Geneva Bible, is an excellent but brief summation of Paul's dissertation: "The great mercy of God is declared towards men in Christ Jesus whose righteousness is made ours through faith."[217]

As is common in first-century letter-writing, the author introduced himself immediately in the first verse of the epistle. He then exulted Christ and the Gospel He came to give us freely by His grace. From Romans 1:6–15, Paul repeatedly refers to his readers and expresses his desire to be with them and minister to them personally.

At that time, Rome was considered the capital of the civilized world and Paul longed to make his presence known there; he also planned to use Rome as a stepping stone to the Iberian peninsula (Romans 15:24–28). The Apostle Paul was always looking for fresh regions to be evangelized.

Romans 1:16–17 present the entire book in capsulized form, and it's worth taking the time to mediate upon and even to commit these verses to memory. When I became a Christian in 1963, Romans 1:16 was one of the first verses I memorized.

Unbelief and its consequences fill out the remainder of the first chapter. Paul reminds us that all of mankind is left without excuse (Romans 1:20), and three times he uses the word *exchange*. In Romans 1:23, sinful man has exchanged God's glory for gross idolatry, in Romans 1:25 the truth is exchanged for a lie, and in Romans 1:26 natural desires are exchanged for *"degrading passions"* (NASB), which leads to an obvious reference to homosexuality and lesbianism in Romans 1:27.

---

[217] *The 1560 Geneva Bible* (Peabody, MA: Hendrickson Publishers, 1969), 70.

The word *sodomy*, named after the city of Sodom in Genesis, is often used interchangeably with homosexuality, which refers to male-to-male sexual activity. The word *lesbian* is named after the ancient Isle of Lesbos off the coast of Greece, which was heavily populated with women who openly sanctioned and practiced sexual acts among themselves. The Greek poetess Sappho lived on this island.

Paul also gives us a catalogue of wicked acts that sinful men and women practice but which God condemns. He takes note of those who not only participate in such sins but also approve of such in others (Romans 1:32).

Knowing there were probably tensions between Jews and Gentiles within the church, Paul stresses in Romans 2:1–16 the impartiality of God. This would come as a shock to even Jewish Christians, who felt they had an edge because they were descendants of Abraham.

With this issue settled, Paul moves on to a discussion of the Law (Romans 2:17–29), which not only is impossible to keep but condemns the Jew who doesn't have saving faith in God, as did Abraham who lived long before the Law was given to Moses on Mount Sinai.

The argument for impartiality is continued into the next chapter and Paul nails it down in Romans 3:9, where we see both Jew and Gentile labour under the burden of sin. The only Scripture Paul knew and preached from was the Old Testament and he backs up his position by drawing from numerous Old Testament scriptures in Romans 3:10–18. Those references include Psalm 14:1–3, 53:1–3, 5:9, 140:3, 10:7, 36:1, and Isaiah 59:7.

With this backdrop, Paul then shuts the door on any person who looks to be justified through the works of the Law (Romans 3:19–20).

## ANALYSIS OF THE GAY AGENDA

The commentary on Romans 1:26–27 in The ESV Study Bible has this to say:

> Not only homosexual acts but also such passions or desires are said to be dishonorable before God. Just as idolatry is unnatural (contrary to what God intended when he made human beings) so too homosexuality is contrary to nature, in that it does not represent what God intended when he made men and women with physical bodies that have a natural way of interacting with each other and natural desires for each other. Paul follows the OT and Jewish tradition in seeing all homosexual relationships, as sinful. The creation account in Genesis 1–2 reveals the divine paradigm for human beings indicating that God's will is for man and woman to be joined in marriage… The sin in view is not pederasty (homosexual conduct of men with boys) but men engaging in sin with men. There is no justification here for the view that Paul condemns only abusive homosexual relationships.[218]

Even modern translations of the Bible have been forced to replace the word *gay* in James 2:3 with an alternative rendering.

The issue of homosexuality is today exacerbated by two realities: (1) a very strong pro-gay movement has made deep inroads into our evangelical churches, and (2) this lifestyle has become politically charged with what can only be described as a militant-like stance.

The English language has been forever changed as a direct result of the pro-gay or same-sex influence. The word gay has been transformed from describing a mood or clothing style to homosexuality. The word *tolerant* used to refer to the ability to accommodate a variety of views, but it has now been changed to mean we must not only endure but also affirm an alternate lifestyle such as homosexuality.

[218] *ESV Study Bible*, 2159.

Christians now face the prospect of being labelled as homophobic or intolerant only because they embrace the clear biblical view of same-sex relationships. This relatively new terminology is explained by Joe Dallas:

> In the manner *homophobia* has been used to tarnish any objection to homosexuality. The word itself is relatively new, coined in 1972 by psychologist George Weinberg, referring to the "dread of being in close quarters with homosexuals." It's meaning has expanded to include, according to Dr. Joseph Nicolos: "Any belief system that values heterosexuality. By that standard, no conservative Christian escapes the homophobic label; religious and non-religious alike."[219]

The pro-gay movement seems desperate to garner the approval of the Bible for their chosen sexual orientation, even to the production of a "gay pride" Bible. Referred to as a new translation to prove that homosexuality isn't condemned in the Scriptures, this new Bible is essentially a mutilation of the text and only proves that with a few changes the scripture can be made to teach whatever we want.

> Homosexual activists, if they address the Bible at all, claim that it is opposed only to forceful and violent homosexual acts, such as rape, and to homosexuality performed in the context of ancient idolatrous temple cults, and that it does not address homosexuality in general and homosexuality in the context of "a loving committed relationship." So the Queen James Bible changes Genesis 19:5 to read "And they called unto Lot,

[219] Joe Dallas, *A Strong Delusion: Confronting the "Gay Christian" Movement* (Eugene, OR: Harvest House, 1996), 135.

and said unto him, Where are the men which came in to thee this night? Bring them out unto us, that we may rape and humiliate them."[220]

This is however, not what the Hebrew says but has simply been changed at will.

Some believers do not have the maturity to deal with this volatile issue in an appropriate manner. I have heard the Adam and Eve, not Adam and Steve joke so often I now cringe every time it is repeated. As Christians we must see the homosexual or lesbian as a person for whom Christ died first and foremost. Thomas Schmidt says it well, "Christians who cannot yet deal with the issues [pertaining to homosexuality] calmly and compassionately, should keep their mouths shut, and they should certainly stay away from the front lines of ministry and public policy debate- not to mention television talk shows.[221]

The movement to have the church sanction homosexuality is very real and most convincing. According to Dallas, there remains an ominous future for the church if the pro-gay agenda is not confronted both in the church and in the public sector.

If the church is unable to resist this movement, it will result in a change of standards in most mainline Protestant denominations—and quite possibly many independent, fundamentalist, evangelical, and charismatic churches. Thus America [and Canada] may one day receive from her own churches, a definition of family standards that include (and approves of) gay marriage, civil protection

[220] *Queen James Bible: The Cornerstone Challenge* (Belmont, MD: Cornerstone Baptist Church, 2013), 3.

[221] Dallas, *A Strong Delusion*, 109.

> for homosexual acts, education (beginning with the primary grades) on the normality of homosexuality, and the general portrayal of same-sex unions as healthy and legitimate.[222]

An even more sinister challenge comes from the paedophile element that sees adults seeking the company of children for sexual gratification. A growing paedophiliac element is making a pitch to change the public perception of what is essentially the exploitation of children. The arguments used by paedophiles to justify their sexual preference are the same as those employed by the pro-gay movement two decades ago. The standard arguments that are proposed, include the following:

- Pedophile is only a problem to those who are distressed over it.
- Societal prejudice creates more anxiety for pedophiles than does their sexuality. Apparently the difficulty is only in the eye of the beholder.
- Pedophiles are no less emotionally stable than anyone else. Their determination is to be seen as normal with natural desires that need to be met.
- Child-adult relationships can be healthy and affirming.[223]

The Christian can only appeal to the Bible for the final answer to these moral issues.

> As with every other sin, the Bible's solution to homosexuality is trusting in Christ for the forgiveness of sin, the imputation of righteousness, and the power to change. After talking about the "sexually immoral" and adulter-

[222] Ibid., 29.

[223] Ibid., 41.

ers and "men who practice homosexuality and "thieves" and "drunkards" (1 Corinthians 6:9–10). Paul tells the Christians, "And such were some of you" (1 Corinthians 6:11). Then he tells them, "But you were sanctified, you were justified in the name of the Lord Jesus Christ and by the Spirit of our God (1 Cor. 6:11; cf. Rom. 6:23, Phil. 2:13; 1 John 1:9). This implies that some former homosexuals in the church at Corinth had left their previous homosexual lifestyle and, by the power of the Holy Spirit, were seeking to live lives of sexual purity whether living celibate lives or in faithful heterosexual marriages.

It is important that the Christian community always show love and compassion toward those engaged in homosexual conduct, and also extend friendship toward them where opportunities arise, though not in a way that signals approval of homosexual practice. It is also important to extend hope for change, since many homosexuals will say they long to establish a different pattern of life...long-term change from a homosexual lifestyle seldom occurs without a program of help and encouragement from others... The moral teachings of God's Word, not people's inward desires, must be the final standard of right and wrong. It is important to recognize that (1) virtually all behaviour is, at some level, biologically influenced and that (2) no command of God is predicated for its validity on humans first losing all desire to violate the command in question.[224]

One well-known magazine has openly attacked the Bible and all who embrace its teachings, especially that which deal with the homosexual issue. Finding Leviticus 20:13 unacceptable

[224] *ESV Study Bible*, 2549.

to a liberal modern world, the writer has chosen to attack the wording of the King James Bible of 1611, which clearly condemns homosexual activity. The same verse in the English Standard Version, which followed the King James Version nearly four hundred years later, has almost the exact same wording. The writer then states that the biblical stance represents a singular moral vision that is ferocious and unacceptable. An increasingly hostile culture has determined to give Bible believers no room for any views that do not meet the sanction of public opinion.[225]

It is probably a true assertion that the Old Testament has been subjected to much more scepticism by critics than the New Testament. In light of this, we must come to terms with "the uncomfortable fact that Jesus often referred to the Old Testament, never distanced Himself from its claims, and affirmed the authority of His apostles whose writings populate the New Testament."[226]

The homosexual issue is addressed in a number of Old Testament passages, and those same teachings are carried over to the New Testament.

> Any intellectually honest look at the Apostle Paul's Greek text in Romans 1:27 reveals the biblical position: Likewise also the men, leaving the natural use of the woman, burned in their lust for one another, men with men, committing what is shameful, and receiving in themselves the penalty of their error which was due.[227]

In one recent article, it was quite astonishing to read that two court rulings in the United States have come out in opposition to those who embrace the Judeo-Christian morality.

[225] Adam Nicolson, "The Bible of King James." *National Geographic*, December 2011, 57.
[226] Craig Parshall, "A More Perfect Union: The Biblical Bottom Line." *Israel My Glory*, November/December 2013, 13.
[227] Ibid.

> Justice Antonin Scalia, in his dissenting opinion, gave Americans fair warning that the decision unfortunately means followers of Judeo-Christian principles—those values located in the Bible—are now considered enemies of the human race.[228]

For the believer, the issue is one of morality based on the Bible:

> Biblical fidelity and the belief in the authenticity and plenary inspiration of Scripture is becoming increasingly important for the church, particularly as America [and Canada] continues its downward slide from being irritably impatient to overtly condemning those who take the Bible seriously. As things progress, the church will be tempted to avoid clearly teaching the Word.[229]

In a world that takes great pains to emphasize love, acceptance, tolerance, and inclusion, we must ask the big questions. Does this include those of us whose worldview is based squarely on the Bible? Does free speech include that part of society that lives by the teachings of the Bible? Or are we to be silenced by those who are offended by the teachings of the Bible?

While we are on the subject of homosexuality, would it be a stretch to ask where the new connotation of the word gay came from? Does the word gay mean anything other than what is already latent in the old-fashioned word homosexuality?

A few words from the writings of David Marshall may help us here. In reference to some modern-day scientists and philosophers, he says,

---

[228] Ibid.

[229] Ibid.

> Why should we care what these or other scientists think about God? (More then, say, union plumbers or minor league catchers?) Scientists are masters of the knowledge that has made the modern world-quarks [in physics, the particles from which protons and neutrons are formed], plate tectonics, genetics, radio waves, medicine.
>
> Few, Dawkins tells us, believe in God. Daniel Dennert has a word to describe this precocious, unbelieving elite: "brights" (modeled on the use of gay to improve the image of homosexuals). A bright is a "person with a naturalist as opposed to a supernaturalist world view," and who possesses an "inquisitive world view.[230]

Regardless of one's view of homosexuality, all have a right to know what has brought us to where we are as a culture.

Another author gives us added insight into a movement that has changed our concept of family as well as our vocabulary. The teaching of the Scriptures in the moral area is in some quarters no longer welcomed as an option:

> The word [gay] suggests a special in-group with access to happiness the rest of us lack. But the important thing this appropriation of an English word achieved for them was tactical control over the public definition of what they are. In the past, you could ask anyone what a homosexual was. But no more. Now, you are expected to defer to a "gay" person to tell you what "gay" and "gay culture" mean. What they now mean is that "within the homosexual subculture, 'gay' is a magical word that has a creative power of its own… the key indicator for today's liberated homosexual," it signifies not simply

[230] David Marshall, *The Truth Behind the New Atheism* (Eugene, OR: Harvest House, 2007), 35.

> those who are attracted to the same sex, but "those who also celebrate this attraction."[231]

Those who defend traditional core values are now forced to a defensive posture. Speaking of the homosexual agenda that has become politically charged and emotionally volatile, William Gairdner notes, "Once they [homosexuals] have defined themselves anew by rejecting society's generic homosexual label and established the 'dignity' of being 'gay,' the next choice was to position normal people as frightened [homophobic], bigoted, and irrational."[232]

The word homophobic, he adds, is now used "like a grenade to throw at anyone who dared to utter the slightest negative opinion."[233] The ultimate goal of the gay agenda is to stifle and silence all opposition.

The last word is given to William MacDonald:

> There is a difference between being a practicing homosexual and having a homosexual tendency. It is practise that God condemns, not the orientation. There are many who have an attraction to their own sex but refuse to give in to it. By the power of the Spirit, they have disciplined themselves to resist the temptation and to live in purity.[234]

Any and all immoral practices are a direct result of the fall in our first parents. Even as Christians, we think evil thoughts and we are tempted in so many ways, but we are urged by God's

---

[231] William D. Gairdner, *The War Against the Family* (Toronto, CA: Stoddart Publishing Company, 1992), 377.

[232] Ibid.

[233] Ibid.

[234] William MacDonald, *Believer's Bible Commentary, Old Testament* (Nashville, TN: Thomas Nelson, 1992), 56.

Word to resist all temptation to sin.

MacDonald continues,

> Christians should accept gays and lesbians as persons without approving their lifestyle. Because they are people for whom Christ died, believers should seek in every possible way to win them to a life of "holiness without which no one will see the Lord." (Heb. 12:14)[235]

There is today a very real danger that free speech and religious liberty will be undermined by strong advocacy groups that want only their view heard, giving no room for alternative options.

Craig Parshall reminds us that in order to stem the tide of what he calls intellectual and moral anarchy Christians will need to know in clear terms "what we believe; why we believe it; and then to make the loving, compelling case for it, even while our opponents rage against us and call us 'haters.'"[236] The perfect role model for all of this is the Lord Jesus Christ.

The following is just one example of how individuals with a biblical worldview are being harassed into silence:

> In the waning weeks of 2013 the Duck Dynasty scandal broke, illustrating again the intolerance toward orthodox Christian idea. Citing the Bible, Duck Dynasty patriarch Phil Robertson voiced his support for traditional marriage and his opposition to homosexuality. His comments went viral, and gay rights protested. So A&E, the channel that airs the family-friendly (and decidedly conservative) program, banned Robertson from the

---

[235] Ibid., 57.

[236] Craig Parshall, "A More Perfect Union: Crimes of the Mind." *Israel My Glory*, March/April 2014, 13.

> show. Because the backlash against A&E was fast and furious, the network relented and negotiated Robertson's apparent return. Yet, the incident proves the willingness of powerful entertainment moguls to submit to dissenters whenever they cry "hate" against Christians.[237]

We are now getting the picture. It is quite acceptable for our culture to entertain words and expression against the Bible, but the culture wants to hear no remarks that support the Bible.

There is no room here to give the homosexual issue the attention it merits in a society where the very mention of such can lead to an emotional firestorm. Many believers are frankly afraid to ever bring the subject into a discussion. Some churches now advise their pastors not to bring homosexuality into the preaching arena, which to me is a major capitulation to a society that has determined to silence all dissenting voices to homosexuality and same-sex marriage. It certainly should be addressed, because it represents a moral issue that is found in both testaments of the Bible and is one of the greatest social and moral issues to impact our culture today.

Authors Gary Bates and Lita Cosner write,

> However, there is a "silver lining" to this cultural crisis. The decline of "cultural Christianity" has sharpened the focus on the differences between real Bible-believing Christians and non-Christians. This actually presents Christians with unprecedented opportunities to share the clear teachings of Scripture and the Gospel, if they are prepared to do so without compromise, and, of course, in a loving manner. Marriage, by definition and by God's design, is a union between a man and a woman. So a homosexual union, whatever else anyone

[237] Ibid.

> may call it, cannot be marriage because it involves two people of the same sex.[238]

Not all Christians feel confident enough to dialogue with those who promote the acceptance of homosexuality in our society, but all believers are obligated to find out what the Bible teaches about this emotionally charged issue.

Pastors need to find the courage of conviction to address this volatile issue in a way that shows respect for God's Word and love for those to whom we minister, including men and women with same-sex orientation. Marriage needs to be addressed from the biblical perspective irrespective of what our culture deems acceptable.

Bates and Cosner further write,

> Whatever the reason for same-sex attraction, justifying it on the basis of some sort of predisposition does not help the individual recognize the ultimate root cause of the problem, which is our natural inborn tendency to sin and break God's laws. This is the ultimate standard by which all actions should be judged.[239]

## JUSTIFICATION BY FAITH

The grand doctrine of justification by faith is the theme of the remainder of Romans 3 as well as the two chapters that follow. Romans 5:1 marks a transition from the doctrine of justification to its application in the life of the believer. The same emphasis is picked up again in Romans 8:28–34.

---

[238] Gary Bates and Lita Cosner, *Gay Marriage: Right or Wrong? And Who Decides?* (Powder Springs, GA: Creation, 2013), 5.

[239] Ibid., 18.

James R White has helped us to simplify our understanding of the doctrine of justification and by faith by allowing the Scriptures to answer the ultimate question. How can a man or woman be made righteous and acceptable in the sight of a holy God? It is this inquiry that Paul labours to address and verbalize.[240]

Romans 3:23 has become standard fare as we prepare ourselves to reach out to the unsaved, and rightly so, but in the context of Paul's teaching this verse and other similar passages need to be taught to Christians now just as they were in Paul's day.

The whole of Romans is a detailed discussion of the Gospel and is addressed to Christians who have become somewhat confused about Gospel content. This epistle isn't so much a preaching mission to the world or a soul-winning manual as it is designed to see Christians deeply grounded in Christian doctrine, especially concerning justification, so that they won't be swayed by every wind of doctrine. Let the blessed Gospel speak for itself.

The Apostle Paul moves into Romans 4 with the sole purpose of proving that what he teaches is evidenced throughout the Old Testament. Paul assures us that Abraham was not justified by works (Romans 4:2) but received right standing with God by faith and faith alone.

Rome was known for its system of law and Paul's readers would have been familiar with such legal words as *justify* and *guilt* (Romans 3:19), which were often used in their court system. Paul sets the table for a courtroom drama when he addresses the guilt of both Jews and Gentiles (Acts 3:9, 19), a verdict that sets us up for the only way a sinner can stand uncondemned in God's courtroom of justice. That way is justification by faith. The faith of Abraham was so strong that even when he, with his wife Sarah at an advanced age, believed he would be given an heir, he became the father of many nations (Romans 4:17–21).

---

[240] James R. White, *The God Who Justifies* (Minneapolis, MN: Bethany House, 2001), 74–76.

The root word for justification is used more than thirty times in Romans and is especially evident from Romans 2:13–5:1. In Romans 3:24, we see the source of our justification, which is grace. In Romans 5:1, we see the means of our justification, which is faith. In Romans 5:9, we see the basis of our justification, which is blood. In Romans 4:2, we see, in contradistinction to the other three references, the negative side of justification, that being that our works are not in any way a factor in finding right standing with God.

Some point out a seeming contradiction between the book of Romans and James 2:24, which states that we are justified by works. But James further explains himself in James 2:26. While Paul dogmatically asserts that we are not saved by works, James emphasizes that saving faith will be evidenced by a transformed life, which is the only tangible way for us to see the faith of a fellow believer. James would argue that a no-works faith is no faith at all, which means there is no justification unless there is evidence of genuine repentance in mind and in life. True faith is active and will be seen not so much for what it is but for what it does.

Building on a justification that is accessed by faith (Romans 5:1), Paul takes us into the results of our justification, including deliverance from the wrath of a holy God (Romans 5:9). In this chapter, Paul builds his case firmly on the first book of the Bible, tracing our need for justification back to the transgression of one man, Adam. Once any doubt is entertained about the literal truthfulness of what happened in the Garden of Eden, the remainder of the Scriptures is destabilized and thrown into disarray. Throughout Romans 5, Paul repeatedly refers to the first man, Adam, and clearly treats the early chapters of Genesis not as myth or allegory but as a factual and literal account (Romans 5:12, 14–15, 17–19).

No less than seventeen times, Paul refers to sin in Romans 6 and draws us into the reality that the Christian life is a daily battle with the nature we were endowed with from conception (Psalm 51:5). We are not given a defeatist mentality here but rather one of victory whereby the believer is responsible to live in everyday life as one who is dead to sin and alive unto God.

This passage ends with another one of those verses that was brought to my attention early in my Christian experience: *"For the wages of sin is death; but the gift of God is eternal life through Jesus Christ our Lord"* (Romans 6:23, KJV).

For the avid Bible reader, Romans 7 is a gold mine for serious study. If you carefully circle or mark in some way the pronouns—such as *I*, *me*, or *my*—there are at least forty-nine to be noted (KJV).

What is seen here is a continuous battle within as the believer is constantly caught between two worlds. Paul desires to deliver the Law from the charge that it is evil in and of itself while at the same time demonstrating that the Law is powerless to keep us from sin.

The key to this text comes from the writings of Douglas J. Moo, who says of Paul, "His basic answer is that the Law though good and holy was given to people who were not."[241] This portion of God's Word deserves far more attention than can be given here, but I will here list the options of interpretation that have been proposed by Bible students who are far more proficient in the Scriptures than yours truly.

- Paul describes his experience as an unconverted Jew under the Law.
- Paul describes his experience, perhaps following his conversion on the Damascus road, as he sought sanctification through the Law in his early Christian walk.
- Paul describes his daily struggle as a mature Christian.[242]

As we approach Romans 8, we are introduced to one of the most impacting portions in all of the Scriptures. The struggle from the previous chapter is still in the picture, but Paul now accents deliverance from sin's bondage, thus freeing us to live a victorious and fulfilling

---

[241] Moo, *Encountering the Book of Romans*, 128.

[242] Ibid., 126–127.

life in the power of the Holy Spirit. The chapter concludes in Romans 8:26–39 with a victory celebration that should cause the praises of God to well up in our hearts. The chapter opened with the Lord Jesus Christ and closed with the same.

Some have viewed Romans 9–11 as a parenthetical section in the book that is sometimes treated as a separate entity, having little connection to the other thirteen chapters. I do not share this assessment. These three chapters are deeply rooted in the first eight chapters of the epistle, especially Romans 2–4 where Jew and Gentile are both found guilty of sin and in need of redemption through the sacrifice of the Lord Jesus on Calvary.

These chapters have been the subject of great controversy, especially the wording of Romans 11:26, which speaks of "all Israel" being saved. As has been the case throughout church history, a great deal depends on how we interpret those passages of Scripture that deal with the church in relation to Israel.

Some are persuaded that Christ went to the cross only after His offer of the kingdom to the Jews was rejected, but the Scriptures are emphatic that His eternal plan was to go to the cross and die for His people (1 John 2:2, 4:14, Revelation 1:5, 13:8). He knew from the beginning that His substitutionary atonement would be mandatory, an absolute necessity, for our redemption. The sacrifice on Calvary wasn't an afterthought in response to a previously failed plan. Calvary was the plan and there could not be, nor would there be, any alternative or substitute for God's agenda. Without the cross, we would be lost for all eternity.[243]

The opening verses of Romans 9 reveal Paul's anguish over the spiritual wellbeing of his fellow Israelites. He appears to be greatly exercised by the fact that the vast majority of his people had rejected their Messiah, and he continued to express his concern in the whole of the next chapter. From Romans 9:7–29, Paul deals with the

---

243 Loraine Bottner, *The Millennium* (Philadelphia, PA: Presbyterian and Reformed Publishing Company, 1970), 219–222.

theological tension that exists between God's sovereignty and human responsibility, a subject that has always stoked the fires of heated discussion among believers of all ages and cultures. Paul does very little to settle the issue or offer any extended explanation.

I am convinced that when we're faced with scriptural teachings that appear to state opposite extremes, we should accept both as equally true and important to God's overall scheme. There is an aura of mystery, it seems to me, into which God has forbidden us to enter and which we fail to fully appreciate because we are human and He is God. This is aptly illustrated in 9:21–23 where God, as the Potter, uses vessels of clay to express either His mercy or His wrath.

Paul's readers in Rome were fully informed that whether they be Jew or Gentile God saw them as members of His church without distinction (Romans 10:12). Further to this, they learn from the very next verse that the invitation to be saved is open to all of their unsaved friends and relatives, too, whether they be Jew or Gentile. In context, this is what Paul is driving home to the church at Rome.

Paul reminds us in the early stages of Romans 11 that though many Jews had rejected their Messiah, a remnant of grace remained. Paul didn't want his Jewish readers to get the impression that God had rejected them entirely, nor did he want to give the Gentiles the impression that they had replaced the Jews in God's affections (Romans 11:3–5).

There continues to be ongoing discussion about Paul's intent in Romans 11:26, where he speaks of all Israel being saved. The following possible interpretations are here given for your consideration:

- The salvation of the church, both Jews and Gentiles, throughout history.
- The saving of a remnant of Jews throughout history.
- The salvation of the end-time generation of Jews in the future over an indeterminate period of time.[244]

---

[244] Moo, *Encountering the Book of Romans*, 171.

Paul ends the chapter with a hymn of praise to God, whose ways are far beyond our understanding (Romans 11:33–36).

Romans 12 begins with a challenge to present our bodies to our Lord as a living sacrifice and not allow ourselves to be fashioned after the thinking and culture of the world in which we live. Every member of the body of Christ is an important and integral part of the whole. Though we live as Christians in what some refer to as the age of grace, Paul gave a number of short and terse commands that remind us there are still laws to be obeyed.

Civil authority is the major topic of Romans 13. Paul reminds us here that God is sovereign even over the civil authorities who call us to accountability concerning the laws of the land. One of the first sermons I preached during ministerial training was based on this chapter. Using the King James Version, I combined verses one and four and applied the title "ordained ministers" to our civil authorities.

Romans 14 encourages Christians to love each other and respect each other's differences. This would certainly be needed in the church of Rome, where Gentiles quite probably outnumbered Jews.

Differences of opinion were to be allowed in what theologians refer to as "a matter of differences," but some believers have zero tolerance for the views of others. While love and unity should always be evident in the body of Christ, an insensitive spirit too often prevails. This is well expressed by Bruxy Cavey:

> *Every conversation demands a certain amount of translation*, because of the simple fact that people use words differently. So watch out. It is possible to get into discussions, debates, and arguments that are not really about anything of *substance* but are more about the *labels* we use to describe our opinions. These arguments about words divide people needlessly, and distract us all from our primary quest for truth.[245]

---

[245] Cavey, *The End of Religion*, 233–234.

The essence of the kingdom is given in Romans 14:17; it's not so much about meat or drink but about peace, righteousness, and the joy of the Holy Spirit. How different and refreshing it would be in our churches if these traits prevailed.

There is a very real tendency for us to fall into the error of the Pharisees whereby prejudges, opinions, traditions, and long-held practices are exalted to a status of authority on par with, or greater than, the Scripture, but with the prejudicial and legalistic way it is sometimes interpreted and applied. The following gives us full warning not to do injustice to fellow believers or the cause of Christ by misappropriating the Word of God:

> "The Pharisees treated their oral Torah as seriously as the written Torah, believing that God gave Moses the oral Torah at the same time as the written Law to help explain, expand, and enhance it (The Mishnah, Abot 1:1). Jesus opposed this view as dangerously exalting the traditions of people to the level of the teachings of God. In other words, the commentary, interpretations, and applications given by the teachers of the Law should be given precedence over Scripture itself. This interpretation leaves the door wide open for human traditions and points of view to be made authoritive in the lives of religious people. In an attempt to remove any mystery from the Bible, religious leaders craft official explanations for every obscure passage and all those explanations, doctrines, and traditions then become sacrosanct. Eventually, those who claim loudest to follow the Bible can end up following their own way instead of God's way."[246]

Romans 15 then takes us to another level by encouraging us to be unselfish and sympathetic to our weaker brother. We are not to exercise a superior attitude toward our brothers and sisters in Christ, and in Romans 15:13 Paul pushes us to be filled with the power of the

[246] Ibid., 249–250.

Holy Spirit. Toward the end of the chapter, Paul anticipates a trip to Jerusalem and expresses his desire to come to Rome as well as to Spain.

From Romans 16:1, we learn that Paul entrusted the delivery of his letter to a woman called Phoebe, a deaconess at the church of Cenchrea, which had probably been established by the nearby church at Corinth. Paul dictated his letter to a man called Tertius (Romans 16:22). In this last chapter of the epistle, he names a number of his fellow workers in the Gospel, then ends the book with a beautiful benediction (Romans 16:25–27).

# The First Epistle of Paul to the Corinthians

The author of this epistle is the Apostle Paul, and the letter was named for the city to which Paul wrote. Ten of Paul's fourteen letters were named for the place to which he wrote. It is widely held that Paul wrote his first letter to the Corinthians from the city of Ephesus, where he ministered for three years. Written around AD 55, Paul anticipated visiting Corinth even as he wrote (1 Corinthians 4:19, 11:34, 16:8).

There are sixteen chapters in the book of 1 Corinthians broken into:

- The Introduction (1:1–9)
- Paul's Appeal for Unity (1:10–17)
- God's Wisdom (1:18–31)
- Meet the Holy Spirit (2:1–16)
- Factions and Foundations (3:1–23)
- Servanthood (4:1–21)
- Immorality and Judgment Within (5:1–13)
- Lawsuits and Liberty (6:1–20)
- Marital Advice (7:1–40)

- Liberty and Licence (8:1–9:27)
- Avoiding the Mistakes of Israel (10:1–33)
- Women and Customs (11:1–16)
- The Lord's Supper (11:17–34)
- Spiritual Gifts (12:1–31)
- Superiority of Love (13:1–13)
- Tongues, Use and Abuse (14:1–40)
- The Resurrection (15:1–58)
- Closing Comments (16:1–24)

## SUMMARY

The city of Corinth, now Gortho, is located in the south of Greece, twenty-five miles west of Athens, and is strategically positioned on a high plateau at the midpoint of a four-mile-wide isthmus providing a land bridge to the rest of Greece. Corinth hosted the Isthmian Games in ancient times, which were second in prominence only to the Olympian Games.

This centre of trade and commerce has been tagged by some as a centre for pagan idolatry, gross immorality, and drunken debauchery, but some writers take the conservative view that this city was little different from other pagan centres of the day.

Corinth was ravaged by the Romans in 146 BC, with shiploads of paintings and art treasures sent to Rome. The city was rebuilt by Julius Caesar in 46 BC, which gave it marketplaces, wide streets, temples, theatres, and fountains. The new construction also provided the blue and white rostra, or bema, where orations were made and judgments rendered. To the south was a steep hill called the Acrocorinth which rose five hundred feet above the city. On this commanding site was located the temple and statue of Aphrodite (Astarte), the goddess of love and fertility.

It was to this heavily populated and prosperous city that the Apostle Paul came about AD 52, preaching Christ and Him crucified, and to which he would write two of his fourteen immortal letters.

Corinth was continuously settled until 1858, when it was decimated by a powerful earthquake that would no doubt have registered high on the modern-day Richter scale. The survivors moved four miles from their ruined city and built the new Corinth. Forty years after the destructive earthquake, excavators began to sift through the nearly buried ruins. Found was a Greek theatre, the temple of Apollo, the agora (marketplace), the bema (judgment platform) before which Paul was brought, and the ancient court and fountain of Peirene. Also uncovered was a forty-six-foot-wide paved street that ran north to south with sidewalks and gutters, a testimony to the advanced engineering skills of the ancient Romans. It has been well said that the Greeks had the brains while the Romans had the drains.[247]

While doctrinal issues relating to sin and righteousness are addressed in Paul's first letter to the Corinthians, his foremost consideration is the correction of behaviour that is badly out of sync with belief. The church in Corinth would present Paul with his greatest challenge, as he was compelled to deal with one problem after another in his first letter to these troubled believers.

Though Paul had been informed by the house of Chloe (1 Corinthians 1:11) that there was bickering among the Christians of Corinth, he addressed them as saints (1 Corinthians 1:2) as well as those who had been sanctified and set apart for God's purposes.

As he prepared to address their many difficulties, Paul reminded them of who they were and assured them he hadn't written them off. His first concern was their lack of unity with the various factions gravitating to different styles of ministry and leadership.

Paul's emphasis on our reliance on the Holy Spirit is his theme in 1 Corinthians 2. Realizing that no believer can make spiritual headway unless enabled by God's power and fully aware of his own dependence on the Holy Spirit, Paul wasted little time getting to our source of victory in this Christian walk. The saints at Corinth were laying the foundation for their spiritual journey on their favourite personalities

---

[247] Tenney, ed., *Zondervan's Pictorial Bible Dictionary*, 182–183.

and making too much of the men who ministered to them. This brought divisions and strife to their local assembly, but Paul pleaded for unity based on their relationship to Christ (1 Corinthians 3:11). Knowing this gave a distorted view of ministry, Paul used the passage in 1 Corinthians 4:1–21 to stress the role of servanthood for all of us, including our leaders.

In 1 Corinthians 5, Paul had to deal with an incestuous relationship that was being tolerated within the local church. One of the men was openly and unashamedly having a sexual and intimate relationship with his own mother, or more probably his stepmother. Paul judged that this man be put out of the church as an example to others that sin would not be sanctioned by the Christian assembly.

Some have wondered about Paul's instruction not to take our brother to court. Are there limitations here? It is my view that Paul was speaking of issues that could be solved within the church without dragging people before a court of law. This certainly doesn't apply to every situation, since heinous transgressions like abuse, rape, and murder (or attempted) must by all means be brought to the civil authorities. And yes, there have been instances when such terrible crimes have been committed by professing Christians. It happens more often than we might think. Paul then made the case that it is sometimes better to accept material or financial loss rather than take a fellow Christian to court (1 Corinthians 6:1–11).

The next chapter presents a detailed discussion about marriage, divorce, and remarriage, a discussion which has provoked no end to heated and continuous controversy. The Christians at Corinth were immersed in a morally impure and extremely permissive culture. Fornication, adultery, polygamy, concubinage, and homosexuality were all freely sanctioned.[248]

Paul addressed many issues raised by the believers, including marriage, celibacy, sexuality, widowhood, and the acceptable response to the social climate. The one topic that is front and centre in this

[248] MacArthur, *The MacArthur Study Bible*, 1737. See notation 1 Corinthians 7:1–11:34.

chapter is that of marriage, between one man and one woman, which is God's only provision for sexual satisfaction and fulfillment. All other options are off-limits for followers of Christ.[249]

This portion of God's Word requires more than a casual read. Liberty and license are the topics of 1 Corinthians 8, and though saved by grace Paul makes plain that we must not ignore the feelings of our brothers and sisters in Christ. Even though we've been set free from the penalty of sin, we have no right to live carelessly.

The early part of 1 Corinthians 9 is occupied with the defence of Paul's apostolic ministry, which was being attacked by some at Corinth. The existence of the church in Corinth, which Paul had founded, was proof enough of the validity of his ministry. Paul clarified the rights of an apostle, including the freedom to marry and the right to receive material support from other believers. Paul protected his integrity by his insistence that his message was free and that he was not owed by anyone.

Sensitivity to the culture of the people to whom he ministered was very much a part of Paul's missionary strategy. This is especially born out of 1 Corinthians 9:19–23, where he purposefully adapts himself to the times and customs of his hearers in order to reach their hearts with the Gospel of Christ.

## DESIRE, DISCIPLINE, AND THE OLYMPIC DREAM

The closing verses of the chapter take us back to the athleticism of the ancient Olympic Games, which are still held every four years. The modern era of the Games was begun in 1896 at Athens, Greece.

Paul drew imagery and illustration from the athletic competitions of the famous Isthmian Games which were held near Corinth. He skillfully used the preparation of runners to

[249] Ibid., 1737. See notations 1 Corinthians 7:2.

teach Christians to approach the Christian life with discipline and self-control. He especially warned of sexual misconduct and other temptations that were a constant danger to Christian leaders, even in today's church. We are starkly reminded of the admonition in Hebrews 12:1 to lay aside any and all sins and hindrances, including overindulgences in legitimate activities, that get in the way of our Christian progress.

Many of us watched in amazement as athletes from around the world competed for medals in the 2012 Olympic Summer Games in London, England. Some of their feats could almost take your breath away. Paul reminds us that these medals are subject to corruption, because they are only material, but Christians strive for a reward or crown that is eternal.

Many Olympic athletes train and practice for their chosen discipline hours and hours nearly every day for four years in order to compete for a medal and claim a few minutes of exhilaration and glory on the world's most prestigious sporting stage. The human stories behind the scenes, as some overcome almost unimaginable obstacles to stake their claim to fame, can elicit our admiration and capture our hearts.

The Apostle Paul helps us to understand that the Christian walk is anything but easy and he urges us to take our example from athletes who make huge sacrifices to enter the competition and strive for the prize.

Images from the London Olympics provide ample testimony to the strength of human endurance, giving us cause to consider whether modern Christians taking their Christianity seriously enough. We could only marvel at the athletic prowess of Jamaica's Usain Bolt as he left all of his competitors behind in the 100-meter final. Canada's Paula Findlay simply fell apart on the track and finished dead last in her event, but she thrilled her fellow Canadians by her sheer grit and determination.

Bridgewater, Nova Scotia native Jenna Martin ran the first heat of her event in the pouring rain, then waited anxiously in that same pouring rain to await the result of her run. You can always spot Jenna at a track meet. Emblazoned on her back are tattooed words from Psalm 56:4, her favourite scripture: "In God I Trust, I will not be afraid." This young athlete truly exemplifies the theme of 1 Corinthians: the grace of God.

Jenna's spiritual journey began early. She says she has always been a Christian, but from the very beginning her faith was greatly tested. Unlike her father and two older brothers, who aren't believers, Jenna's mother is a Christian who took her to Sunday school and services at the Baptist Church. There, with her father looking on, thirteen-year-old Jenna and her mother went through the waters of baptism together.

From her early childhood, Jenna developed a love for sports and athleticism, and by the age of twelve she knew she could run fast and began breaking records.

Her spiritual life took a nosedive during her days in college. With her parents separated, and now on her own, she turned to drinking and partying while academics and athletics became less important. She also abandoned her faith, but God did not abandon her. Following a year of living in a very unhappy state, Jenna met her future husband, whose positive influence led to the restoration of her faith. Her academics and athletic pursuits were renewed, along with fresh enthusiasm for church attendance and Bible reading.

The road to the London Olympics was a bumpy ride for this small-town girl. Prior to the Games, she moved to Florida to hone her skills in her chosen discipline, the 400-meter. Jenna saw the dark side of her long-time coach at this time and she was deeply hurt by someone she had trusted and thought she knew. The fallout from this painful experience is still being felt as Jenna struggles with closure and forgiveness. Her refreshing honesty is the most impressive part about her testimony.

There is a brighter side here. While in Florida, and in the throes of personal trauma, she found a spiritual refuge at the Celebration of Praise Church in Clermont. She was warmly embraced by this church family, and in the midst of distress and disillusionment she had a profound experience with the Holy Spirit. She found new strength in anticipation of the Olympics, and became determined to run for God's grace and glory. She qualified for a place on Canada's Olympic team in her last chance to do so and sensed God's presence as she ran the last straightaway.

Jenna's tattoo sends the message that God always has our back, but this committed Christian isn't looking back, only ahead. Falling short of the medal round in London, she set her sights on the 2016 games in Rio but failed to make the cut. In the eyes of Canadians, she was already a gifted and proven athlete as well as a national heroine. In 2012, she was the Canadian national champion in the 400-metre and is Nova Scotia's best-ever 400-metre runner. On March 31, 2015 she was married to DeQuin Evans, a professional athlete in his own right.

Following the 2016 Olympic Games, Martin-Evans retired from athletic competition on the track. In 2017, she made a bid to become part of Canada's bobsleigh team with a view to competing at the Winter Olympics planned for Pyeongchang in 2018.

Whatever lies ahead for this talented athlete, we know she will have a positive impact for the Gospel of Christ. We wish her every success.

The translators of the Geneva Bible draw a lesson from the fierce competition that is evident in our own modern games:

> The Apostle calleth them by a pleasant similitude, and also by his own example, to sobriety and mortification of the flesh, showing that they cannot be fit to run or wrestle... which pamper up their bodies, and therefore affirming that they can have no reward, unless they take another course and trade of life.[250]

The scriptures tell us in Proverbs 24:16 that a righteous man (or woman) may fall seven times, but he (or she) continues to get up again. Success is not measured by how many times we fall, but by how many times we rise to our feet again.

Tiki Gelana of Ethiopia literally saved the best for last in the women's marathon. As she entered the second half of her race and reached for her water bottle, she collided with another runner and fell to the ground. Her right elbow got scraped, but stood up and almost immediately was bumped a second time. She won that race in record time, leaving her closest rivals from Kenya and Russia behind as she roared across the finish line.

Christians who fall and fail often forget that the prize before us is yet attainable. Hebrews 12:1–2 says we are to run the race with endurance and keep our eyes fixed and focused on our Lord Jesus Christ.

Take a lesson from this Ethiopian runner who simply refused to quit. If you fall down in your Christian walk, get up again and keep keeping on. We all get bumped and bruised along the way and temptation stalks us at every corner. Let us encourage one another to be all that God intended as we run the race and pursue the prize.

---

[250] *The 1599 Geneva Study Bible*, 1177. See notation 1 Corinthians 9:24.

1 Corinthians 10 gives us a dire warning not to condone or copy the sins of the Israelites in the Old Testament, whom Paul uses as an example of what not to do in the Christian life.

The differing roles of men and women are then dealt with in 1 Corinthians 11, and the head covering issue is seen in light of the custom of the day (1 Corinthians 11:2–16).

The ancient city of Corinth was known for its pagan temple of Aphrodite where as many as one thousand prostitutes were housed and sold their services. Their hair was cropped short, which was unbecoming of a modest woman of that time, and they wore no head covering. When one of these priestesses was converted, she wasn't allowed in the Christian place of worship without a head covering to distinguish her from the temple prostitutes. The Christian women of the time were all instructed to either wear a head covering or, barring that, wear their hair long.

When a temple prostitute became a Christian, it took a while for her hair to grow, so in the meantime she was asked to wear a head covering. This instruction was obviously tailored to address the local custom in Corinth and Paul asked the Christians not to be contentious about it (1 Corinthians 11:16).[251]

This is an example of how the Scriptures can be twisted out of all proportion when taken out of context and removed from their cultural setting. There is no instruction here for women never to cut their hair or to wear a hat to a worship service.

The most controversial passage of this epistle is undoubtedly 1 Corinthians 12–14, which has often caused a deep divide among Christians. Most Christians come to these chapters with a prejudicial mindset due to their particular denominational slant or spiritual upbringing. We need to recognize that there are sincere and godly Christians on all sides of the issue and we can all learn from each other.

1 Corinthians 12 is chiefly occupied with the spiritual gifts:

---

[251] *Liberty Bible Commentary*, 2312–2313.

> Spiritual gifts are divine enablements for ministry that the Holy Spirit gives in some measure to all believers and that are to be completely under His control and used for the building of the church to Christs' glory… These had to be distinguished from the mystical experiences called "ecstasy" (supernatural, sensuos communion with a diety) and "enthusiasm" (divination, dreams, revelations, visions) that were found in the pagan religions of Corinth.[252]

In another notation, MacArthur comments on 1 Corinthians 12:4: "These categories of giftedness are not natural talents, skills, or abilities, such as are possessed by believers and non-believers alike."[253]

Richard Dortch reminds us how easy it is to abuse our gifts:

> We speak of the power of the Holy Spirit, and rightly so, for in Him resides the power behind the gifts of the Spirit. Yet when he bestows a particular gift that person sometimes acts as if it were his use [or her] for his own benefit. That is spiritual pride in its worst form.[254]

However, the following should be noted:

- There are a variety of spiritual gifts, all given by the Holy Spirit.
- All members of the body are valuable for the working of the whole.
- Not all believers have the same gifts.
- No gift is more needful or important than another.
- No believer is allowed bragging rights in the exercise of their gift.
- All members of the body are to exemplify the excellency of love as presented in 1 Corinthians 13.

---

[252] MacArthur, *The MacArthur Study Bible*, 1746–1747. See notation 1 Corinthians 12:1.

[253] Ibid., 1747. See notation 1 Corinthians 12:4.

[254] Richard W. Dortsch, *Fatal Conceit* (Green Forest, AR: New Leaf Press, 1993), 170.

1 Corinthians 13:1–13 is the link that connects the entire discussion of gifts in 1 Corinthians 12 with the 1 Corinthians 14, which features the abuse of the gift of tongues. This portion is certainly one of the most beloved in all of Scripture and is worthy of much study and meditation by all believers.

Some could capably argue that 1 Corinthians 13 is the most powerful chapter in the entire Word of God. What follows is the Cotton Patch Version of this chapter, which is the work of Clarence Jordan. This passage sums up the scriptural reality that whatever we are or whatever we do, our driving principle must always be the love of God, which is shed abroad in our hearts by the Holy Spirit.

> Though I speak with the tongues of men and of angels, but have no love, I am a hollow-sounding horn or a nerve-wracking rattle. And though I have the ability to preach, and know all the secrets and all the slogans, and though I have sufficient faith to move a mountain, but have no love, I am nothing. Even though I renounce all my possessions, and give my body as a flaming sacrifice, but have not love, I accomplish exactly nothing. Love is long-suffering and kind. Love is not envious, nor does it strut and brag. It does not act up, not try to get things for itself. It pitches no tantrums, keeps no books on insults or injuries, sees no fun in wickedness, but rejoices when truth prevails. Love is all-embracing, all-trusting, all-hoping, all-enduring. Love never quits. As for sermons, they shall be silenced; as for oratory, it shall cease; as for knowledge, it will vanish. For our knowledge is immature, and our preaching is immature; but when that which is mature arrives, it supersedes the immature. For example, when I was a child, I was talking like a child, thinking like a child, acting like a child, but when I became an adult, I outgrew my childish ways. So, on the childish level (i.e., *without love*) we look at one another in a trick mirror, but on the adult level (i.e., *with love*) we see face to face; as a child

> [i.e. *without love*] I understood immaturely, but as an adult [i.e., *with love*] I'll understand just as I'll be understood. Now, these three things endure: faith, hope and love; but the greatest of all is love. Seek diligently for love.[255]

My discussion of 1 Corinthians 14 will be somewhat limited, and its content is worthy of far more attention than is here given.

Over the years, I have heard my share of heated discussions about the contents of this particular passage. Bring together some dogmatic Brethren Assembly people, some diehard Pentecostals, and throw in some dyed-in-the-wool Baptists and you have the recipe for a red-hot emotional firestorm.

The major issues of the chapter are essentially two: tongues and interpretation, and the place of women in the local church. In my experience, much of the discussion arising from this chapter generates more heat than light. Since the two issues presented are vitally connected in the chapter, they must be seen as parts of a whole, which really comes down to order within the local assembly.

The matter of tongues as given in this chapter seems to have arisen from the abuse of this gift in the church of Corinth. Throughout church history, there seems to have been periodic manifestations of this gift among those who traditionally haven't been seen as Pentecostal or Charismatic. On the other hand, I have met a number of Pentecostal people who, though born and raised in a Charismatic atmosphere, have never experienced the gift of tongues.

## ORDER VERSUS CONFUSION

Paul lays out some clear guidelines for the manifestation of tongues in the local assembly. No more than three people are to exercise the gift of tongues in any one meeting and they are to speak each in turn and

---

[255] *Cotton Patch Version of Paul's Epistle* (New York, NY: New York Association Press, 1968), 66–67.

not together (1 Corinthians 14:27). There is to be interpretation of what is said, and if no interpreter is present there is to be silence in the assembly (1 Corinthians 14:27–28). Instructions are also given in 1 Corinthians 14:29–32 for those who prophesy.

The crux of the chapter is 1 Corinthians 14:33, which addresses the confusion and disorder that had come to characterize the worship services of the church at Corinth. It is in this context that we look at the next two verses, where Paul specifically tells women to be silent.

Whatever you have been taught about these verses, it is probably far removed from the intent of the Apostle Paul. This is not the first time in the epistle that Paul has told someone to keep silent. In 1 Corinthians 14:28, which seems to refer more to men, they are told to be silent when there is no one to interpret when someone speaks in tongues. In the same context, he later tells the women to be silent, but he adds an additional thought in 1 Corinthians 14:35 which seems to clearly address married women.

From 1 Corinthians 14:33–40, the issue is not men versus women, but rather order versus confusion. Some Christian groups have taken these verses totally out of context, giving men the authority to keep women from exercising any ministry in the local church. The only issue Paul is concerned with here is the issue of tongues and its abuse in the Corinthian church.

Across the bay from Corinth was Delphi, famous in Greece as a centre for oracles. There, individuals came to an enclosure and some of the men were chosen by lot to enter the inner sanctum where they could consult their god. Women were not allowed into this private domain. Once in the confines of this sacred shrine, the men were met with a woman who sat on a tripod and, while inhaling fumes from a deep chasm, became intoxicated (supposedly) and spoke in an incoherent tongue to give a message to the inquirer from the god. A priest or priestess would then interpret the message for the inquirer.

Modern research has suggested that these fumes were probably acidic sulphuric gases emanating from underground streams below the chasm. Paul was fully aware of this Delphic oracle and there is no doubt the Corinthian Christians were being affected by this ancient practice and had carried over some of its excesses into the local assembly.[256]

Another influence on the minds of the Corinthians would have been the various mystery cults that were an integral part of Greek religious life. The most famous were the Eleusinian mysteries centred in the city of Eleusis, which for a time rivalled the nearby city of Athens for splendour and prominence. Welcoming visitors from all over Greece and beyond, this city boasted a temple precinct that survived for more than a thousand years.[257]

The temple was built and rebuilt after being destroyed several times. Into this sacred edifice, inductees entered the Hall of Mysteries, from where they were guided to underground caverns. They then were led through religious ceremonies that were sure to be kept secret from the outside world. To this day, we know very little about what transpired here.[258] The worshipers were assured they would thrill with new revelations and be mysteriously united with God in oneness.[259] Some verses in Paul's letter would remind them of the mysterious (1 Corinthians 4:1, 13:2, 15:2, 15:51).

Paul was concerned that confusion not be a part of Christian worship and found that some of the young married women were interfering with order in the assembly by constantly interfering with the men in the service. Being fully conversant with the goings-on at the oracle of Delphi, some of the women began to act like the priestesses of Delphi and, mistakenly thinking they had the gift of tongues and interpretation, actually pushed the men aside in the service. Using his apostolic authority Paul ordered these women to ask their questions

---

[256] Will Durant, *The Life of Greece* (New York, NY: Simon and Schuster, 1966), 104–105, 197–199.

[257] Charles Freeman, *Egypt, Greece, and Rome* (New York, NY: Oxford University Press, 1966), 125.

[258] Ibid., 192–193.

[259] Durant, *The Life of Greece*, 189.

at home rather than create havoc in the church. The Corinthian church was the only one in the New Testament where tongues and interpretation were addressed by the Apostle, and only because of their abuse and resultant confusion.

Some passages of Scripture deal with specific issues and have become well known for their particular emphasis. 1 Corinthians 13 is known as "the love chapter," and two chapters later we are introduced to the most detailed treatment of the resurrection in all of Scripture. Having dealt with present difficulties elsewhere in his epistle, Paul ends on an upbeat and positive note. The fifty-eight verses of 1 Corinthians 15 serve as Paul's summa cum laude for the resurrection, and it would be incomplete without this powerful passage of God's Word being included.

1 Corinthians 15:4–6 offer a creedal statement made in a culture of religious pluralism, which makes it as relevant today as it was in the first century. Paul's uncompromising position toward the idolatrous practices of Corinth needs to be heard in our present day. Idols are as nothing and there is only one true and living God.[260] The New Bible Commentary states, "Christians are not simply theists. For them, there is only one Lord Jesus Christ and he is the agent of all that is created."[261]

1 Corinthians 15:29 has sparked no end to discussion. This is one of the most controversial verses in all of Scripture. The following is a quote from the New Geneva Study Bible:

> Apparently some in Corinth were being baptized on behalf of others who had already died. This practice is not mentioned elsewhere in the Bible or in any other ancient writings. Numerous explanations of the practice have been proposed, all of them speculative and none persuasive. Paul mentions the rite only to show the logical inconsistency of his opponent's position.[262]

---

[260] Compare Deuteronomy 6:4 and Isaiah 40:25–26.

[261] *The New Bible Commentary*, 1174.

262 *New Geneva Study Bible*, 1821.

After sounding a note of victory in 1 Corinthians 15:57, Paul brings his letter to a close. He comments on how financial support is to be handled, what his immediate plans entail, and then gives a final exhortation along with closing greetings and a solemn farewell.

## PONDERING PENTECOSTALISM

The events recorded in Acts 1 and 1 Corinthians 12–14 demand more than a passing glance. This is largely due to the renewed interest in the supernatural manifestation of speaking in tongues (glossolalia) that began in the early years of the twentieth century. This phenomenon is the most characteristic trait of those modern-day churches that are termed Pentecostal or Charismatic, but it certainly isn't confined to them.

This delicate issue has often given rise to heated arguments and supercharged verbal exchanges, making it virtually impossible for some Christians to maintain any kind of meaningful fellowship. Perhaps it is time for Christians of all persuasions to lower their rhetoric and engage in open and candid discussion about a topic that is almost always explosive.

In deference to pursuing a full-blown discussion of this issue, I here offer some thoughts about Pentecostalism in general and the matter of tongues in particular.

I am glad to say that Pentecostal people represent, by and large, a movement of Bible believers who are for the most part very devoted Christians. I have never met any Pentecostal people who have been swayed by modernistic theology. They embrace the great fundamentals of the faith, including the deity of Christ, the inspiration of the Scriptures, blood atonement, and salvation by grace alone.

One branch of Pentecostals is commonly called Jesus-Only Pentecostals and deny the teaching of a triune God. They are considered aberrant and cultic even by mainline Pentecostals.

Long-time pastor of the First Baptist Church of Atlanta, Georgia, Charles Stanley, has made this thought-provoking statement:

> In some churches there is an invisible caste system. There are those who claim to have the sign gift of tongues and those who do not. That is totally unscriptural. When people say the "haves have spoken in tongues and the "have nots" have not spoken in tongues they set up a harmful division between Spirit-filled believers.[263]

Stanley was raised in a Pentecostal home and is very sensitive to the feelings of Pentecostal Christians.

While the tongues in Acts appear to be similar to whatever was going on in Corinth, there is a decided difference. The tongues in Acts were fully controlled by the Holy Spirit while the corresponding events in the Corinthian Church (1 Corinthians 14) were more in the hands of the participants, and because of abuse had to be regulated. This begs the question, how do you place restrictions on a miracle? Paul did just so, and stated that his instructions were the commandments of God (1 Corinthians 14:37).

Some writers in the past and present, including Jerry Jensen, have reported that great men of the past, such as D.L. Moody and Charles Finney, have testified of speaking in other tongues. Not one shred of evidence can be found to substantiate these claims. Neither they nor their biographers have ever laid claim to such. To infer that they did when they obviously didn't is both manipulative and misleading.

---

[263] Charles Stanley, *The Glorious Journey* (Nashville, TN: Thomas Nelson, 1996), 57.

Possibly no individual has published more of Moody's sermons than John R. Rice, but there is no proof that the great Chicago preacher ever experienced speaking in tongues. He does tell how "he was filled with the Holy Spirit after he had pleaded for God's power for some time and how many were saved there-after." He called his experience the baptism with the Holy Spirit, which is synonymous with the filling of the Spirit.[264] Rice adds, "In America, Charles G. Finney was wonderfully baptized with the Holy Spirit and said so but he did not talk in tongues."[265]

This next quote comes from author Herb Vander Lugt, of RBC Ministries:

> Regrettably, tongues have become a source of confusion and division among many well-meaning Christians. This is partly because some tongues speakers declare it to be a necessary companion to the baptism of the spirit—and see Christians who don't speak in tongues as deficient in spiritual experience. But the fire of this controversy is also fanned by an over-reaction on the part of some non-charismatics.[266]

Some Bible scholars, especially of the dispensational school of thought, have for many years used 1 Corinthians 13:8–13 to prove that it would be impossible for the miracle of tongues to take place today. Some of that mindset, including Lugt, have softened their view and suggest that the passage, and more particularly the expression *"when that which is perfect is come"*

---

264 John R. Rice, *The Charismatic Movement* (Murfreesboro, TN: Sword of the Lord Publishers, 1977), 79.

265 Ibid., 79.

266 Herb Vander Lugt, *What About Speaking in Tongues?* (Grand Rapids, MI: RBC Ministries, 2001), 4.

(1 Corinthians 13:10, KJV), is not conclusive. Some writers see the expression as a reference to the eternal state, which resonates positively with me.[267]

From the first century of our era until the early part of the last century, tongues were virtually unknown among believers. Are we to believe that the church was blindsided for nineteen centuries and that God allowed His people to live and die without His power for the best part of two thousand years? Pentecostals T.B. Barratt and George Jeffreys, along with the leaders of the European Pentecostal Conference of 1939, are among those who have publicly acknowledged that tongues is not the only evidence of the Spirit baptism.[268]

Pentecostals themselves admit there are excesses within their movement, which prompts the question, why are these excesses allowed to continue? The tongues experience is dying on this continent. According to an article in *Christianity Today* some time ago, many Pentecostal pastors in the United States see the emphasis on tongues as a barrier to soul-winning as well as outreach to Christians looking for a home church. Some have gone so far as to suggest that the tongues issue should be removed from their doctrinal statement.

That same publication reported that many younger Pentecostal preachers do not view tongues with the same vigour as their senior forebearers.[269] The trend to placing less emphasis on tongues is noted by C. Peter Wagner:

> Many second-generation Pentecostal leaders embarrassed by their parents' exuberance and by the label "Holy Rollers" have determined to make their churches more respectable. Surveys show for example, that a large

[267] Ibid., 22–23.

[268] Ibid., 71.

[269] Cary McMullen, "Holding Their Tongues." *Christianity Today*, October 2009, 15–19.

percentage of US Pentecostal members do not speak in tongues.[270]

From a positive standpoint, the worship style of many churches has changed in response to the influence of Pentecostalism. Our Pentecostal friends have taught us how to worship with our entire being, including uplifted hands, swaying bodies, moving feet, and upbeat music punctuated with verbal affirmations such as "Amen," "Praise the Lord," "Thank You, Jesus," and "Hallelujah." Many have adopted the more contemporary style of worship, which has attracted followers from the younger generation.

Sometimes interpretation is absent in a Pentecostal service, which means there is no understanding of what is being said by the remainder of the congregation.[271] Often the music is loud and lively, with a leader repeatedly encouraging people to "seek and speak" (tongues). This kind of undue pressure and manipulative technique is foreign to the Scriptures. It also brings confusion to the minds of any unconverted who may be present, who are left wondering what it really means to be a Christian.

It could be capably argued that in many Christian quarters the ministry of the Holy Spirit has been largely ignored. With their strong emphasis on the third person of the triune God, Pentecostal people stand as a reminder of our need of God's power in our lives.

Pentecostal Christians who wonder why other believers are somewhat sceptical of their emphasis on tongues need to consider how they are perceived by others. It is easy to see why Christians of other persuasions feel alienated by Pentecostals. John R. Rice expresses it well for many, as he speaks of the

[270] Wagner, *Dominion!*, 110–111.

[271] Compare this scenario with Acts 2:4–8 and 1 Corinthians 14:5–28.

Pentecostal brand of Christianity: "They say that only those who talk in tongues have the fullness of The Spirit. Thus they claim to be better Christians than all the great soul-winners of the ages who did not talk in tongues."[272]

Any attitude that even remotely betrays pride or arrogance, though unintended, sends a negative message to other Christians. Tony Evans shares the same concerning the equality of believers:

> The point then is that all converts in Acts receive full membership in the church, even though word of the fulfillment of the promise took some time to get around. There were no believers in Acts relegated to the back of the spiritual bus. There were no second-class Christians then, and there are none today.[273]

The third chapter of 1 Timothy is largely a list of qualifications for pastors and deacons. This fairly comprehensive summary is often the starting point for churches who seek worthy individuals for local church ministry. The matter of *"the husband of one wife"* (1 Timothy 3:2) has provoked a certain degree of controversy in some quarters. There are churches and ministries who insist that divorced men are disqualified from ministry regardless of the circumstances, while others see this issue differently.

With this lone exception, the remaining qualities are easily understood. We also note that speaking in tongues is absent from this passage in 1 Timothy.

The question that begs to be asked, especially of those who insist that tongues is the initial evidence of the filling of the Holy Spirit, is this: how can it be that the issue of tongues is absent

---

[272] Rice, *The Charismatic Movement*, 77.

[273] Tony Evans, *The Promise* (Chicago, IL: Moody Press, 1996), 52.

in portions of Scripture that target the minimal requirements for effective ministry? In 1 Timothy 3, a chapter that entails the basic expectations of Christian leadership, tongues fails to make the short list.

# The Second Epistle of Paul to the Corinthians

**The author of this epistle is the Apostle Paul, who probably wrote it after** he left Ephesus and before he arrived in Corinth in AD 55. There are thirteen chapters in the book of 2 Corinthians broken into:

- The Introduction (1:1–11)
- The Integrity of Paul (1:12–24)
- Love Reaffirmed (2:1–17)
- Ministry and the New Covenant (3:1–18)
- Paul's Apostolic Ministry (4:1–18)
- Temporal versus the Eternal (5:1–21)
- The Cost of Ministry (6:1–12)
- Separation (6:13–18)
- The Heart of Paul (7:1–16)
- Generosity (8:1–24)
- Giving Cheerfully (9:1–15)
- The Transparency of Paul (10:1–18)
- Paul's Apostleship Defended (11:1–23)

- The Visionary Paul (12:1–21)
- Self-Examination (13:1–14)

## SUMMARY

With the exception of Philemon, this is Paul's most personal letter. In contrast to his first letter to the Corinthians, this second epistle is much less doctrinal and more personal and emotional. At the time of writing, Paul's ministry was under severe attack, which gives this epistle a feeling of defensiveness as he shares some of his more personal experiences, including his own weaknesses and temptations.

As Paul opens his letter, he is very conscious that the saints in Corinth are looking for a personal visit and he reaffirms his promise made earlier. He touches on his first epistle in 2 Corinthians 2 and assures them that this letter will not be as severe as the first. There is no apology for what he said, though, since it was necessary; but he wouldn't address the same issues again. Paul expresses his continued love for his brothers and sisters in Corinth and then emphasizes his sincerity and deep concern for them.

In the third chapter, Paul discusses his role as a minister of the new covenant, and in 2 Corinthians 3:17, he brings our attention to the liberty that is found wherever the Holy Spirit is present.

Regarding 2 Corinthians 4, John MacArthur reminds us,

> God makes it clear that salvation is the result of His power and not any power His messengers can generate (cf. 2:16) the great power of God overcomes and transcends the clay pot. The messenger's weakness is not fatal to what he does; it is essential (cf. 12:9–10).[274]

The fifth chapter presents the contrast between that which is temporal with that which is eternal. Paul is far more concerned with

[274] MacArthur, *The MacArthur Study Bible*, 1769. See notation 2 Corinthians 4:7.

what is in the heart than what is seen on the outside (2 Corinthians 5:12). Later descriptions of Paul in other writings have suggested that he was a hunchback, quite short, bald-headed, and not in any way attractive in appearance.[275]

The high cost of ministry is addressed in 2 Corinthians 6 as Paul reminds us that true Christian service is no glamour trip but is rather filled with hardship and difficulty. Later in the chapter, he warns us about entanglements that may jeopardize or compromise our testimony, including marriage to unbelievers.

Reference to afflictions Christians face is made in 2 Corinthians 7:5, where he speaks of the fears we experience within and the conflicts we face without.

Stressing the greatness of generosity in 2 Corinthians 8, Paul uses Christ as our supreme example who became poor so that we might become rich. This theme is continued in the next chapter as the apostle illustrates his view of giving with the principle of sowing and reaping (2 Corinthians 9:6).

## PAUL'S THORN IN THE FLESH

Paul becomes very personal in 2 Corinthians 10, where he again contrasts one's outward appearance with what comes from the heart as one shares the Gospel of Christ with a needy world (2 Corinthians 10:10–12, 16).

Some questioned Paul's leadership and authority, and Paul defends his position in 2 Corinthians 11. He also sounded a warning about some who were posing as apostles but were in reality Satan in disguise (2 Corinthians 11:13–15).

Paul's vision of paradise in the opening verses of 2 Corinthians 12 has made for much discussion as to when he saw the vision and whether he was dead at the time and then raised from the dead, or was in an unconscious state. Even Paul himself did not know (2 Corinthians 12:2).

---

[275] Herbert Lockyer, *All the Men in the Bible* (Grand Rapids, MI: Zondervan, 1974), 270.

Much discussion has also been made of the thorn in the flesh Paul speaks of in 2 Corinthians 12:7–9. We simply do not know, but I give here the possibilities that have been entertained among Christian writers:

- Sexual temptation.
- Opposition from others.
- An abrasive or opinionated nature.
- A bodily affliction (possibly poor eyesight).
- Poor speech.

The final chapter finds Paul reasserting his authority and closes with benedictions and personal greetings (2 Corinthians 13:11–14).

# The Epistle of Paul to the Galatians

Galatia was a Roman province which embraced a large chunk of what is now modern-day Turkey. The people of that area were called Galatians and these are the people to whom the letter is addressed. The letter appears to have been addressed to Christians throughout that area rather than to one specific church. This letter may have been written in AD 49, but the date is still debated by scholars.

The author of Galatians was the Apostle Paul, and there are six chapters in the epistle broken into:

- Introduction (1:1–5)
- The Gospel Perverted (1:6–24)
- The Council of Jerusalem (2:1–10)
- Peter Rebuked (2:11–21)
- Faith and Righteousness (3:1–14)
- The Law's Intent (3:15–29)
- Sonship (4:1–20)
- Sarah and Hagar (4:21–31)

- Walking in the Spirit (5:1–26)
- Bearing Burdens (6:1–18)

## SUMMARY

The key to understanding the epistle at hand is to, first of all, recognize the fickle temperament of the people to whom Paul was writing. Secondly, we need to understand that the issue of this letter has to do primarily with the relationship between Law and grace. These people had been evangelized by Paul during his first missionary journey, and since that time traditional Jewish teachers had been sowing seeds of doubt among the Gentile converts about the place of the Law in their Christian experience. The Jews, even some who had been converted, had been rejecting the apostolic teaching of salvation by grace alone and were busily promoting Law-keeping among these converts in Galatia.

In Galatians 4:13–16 and Acts 14:8–9, we see the temperamental nature of these converts as they appear to become overwhelmed by these very persuasive Jews, leaving Paul with the colossal task of keeping them grounded in their newfound faith.

From the outset of this epistle, we see the serious nature of what is transpiring among these Galatian churches as the Gospel had been changed and even replaced by another message altogether (Galatians 1:1–3). Later in the first chapter, Paul was forced once again to defend his ministry as he had with the Corinthians.

Things had deteriorated so badly that even the Apostle Peter had to be soundly rebuked by Paul, because he had held himself aloof from the Gentiles in Antioch when his Jewish brethren had arrived from Jerusalem. Even Barnabas had wavered as a result of Peter's actions (Galatians 2:11–14).

Paul had to address all who would endeavour to bring these Gentile converts under the Law of Moses. With continued emphasis on the Old Testament Scriptures, and using Abraham as an example of salvation by faith, Paul continued to chisel away at the inroads made by the Judaizers.

In the latter part of Galatians 3, Paul summoned all of his persuasive and intellectual powers in order to keep his converts from slipping away from the Gospel. He explains the true intent of the Law, which is to be a schoolmaster bringing us to Christ. He then informs us of our adoption, or sonship, in Christ, after which he uses Sarah and Hagar to help us grasp that Law is bondage and grace is freedom. Paul doesn't throw out the moral Law, but he teaches strongly that power and victory over sin is not achieved by trying to keep the Law but by trusting in the power of the Holy Spirit.

> By means of the ceremonial law, God speaks in picture language of the salvation He was to effect through the life and death of the Incarnate Son. Of necessity, therefore, it was but imperfect and temporary. The social legislation governing Israel was designed for particular culture at a given period of history so it, too, was but for a time, yet the principles which underlay it are timeless and applicable to all generations. God's moral law is enforced everywhere and at all times, for it is a reflection of His very being. It has never been abrogated, nor indeed can be.[276]

The manifold fruit of the Holy Spirit is listed in Galatians 5:22–23, and they should characterize our walk with the Lord.

The epistle then closes with two types of burden-bearing being addressed (Galatians 6:1–6). In Galatians 6:15, Paul leaves no doubt that circumcision has nothing to do with being a Christian; the real fruit is a changed life.

> Wherever religion has lost its reality, wherever ritual is more regarded than right living, wherever subscription to a creed is substituted for submission to Christ, wherever loud claims

---

[276] Tenney, ed., *Zondervan's Pictorial Bible Dictionary*, 480.

of orthodoxy are accompanied by conduct devoid of charity, wherever deeds of self-righteousness are obscuring the glory of the cross, there this epistle should be made to a new dependence upon justifying grace, to a faith that is shown by works, to a walk that is by the Spirit, to a life inspired by love.[277]

[277] *Liberty Bible Commentary*, 2369.

# Conclusion: A Story of Amazing Grace

Paul's epistle to the Galatians is the last of the nine New Testament books discussed in this first part of *Odyssey of Grace*. In bringing this volume to its conclusion, I will share the compelling testimony of one man's quest for acceptance before God following a titanic emotional struggle that results in his marvellous conversion to Christ.

Born in Belfast, Ireland in 1898, Clive Staples Lewis was the youngest brother and only sibling to Warren (Warnie), who had been born three years earlier to their parents, Albert and Flora Lewis.

By the age of five, with a brashness beyond his years, Clive informed his parents that he would answer only to the name Jacksie, thereby dismissing his given name, which he despised. Later, his adopted name was modified to Jacks, or Jack.

The Lewis household abounded with a plentiful supply of books, which greatly enhanced Jack's natural appetite for reading and the pursuing of an academic career. From 1925 to 1954, he lectured at

Oxford University, followed by a shorter tenure at Cambridge from 1954–1963.[278]

In 1956, Lewis married the recently divorced Joy Davidman Gresham, a Jewish American, who brought two young sons from her previous marriage. This aspiring poet and novelist had been converted to Christ shortly after the Second World War had ended. Four years following her marriage to Lewis, she succumbed to the ravages of cancer.[279]

People of faith have struggled with complexities and contradictions that dogged C.S. Lewis for most of his adult life. Excesses in his personal life including crudeness of speech and a lifelong passion for tobacco and liquor that continued unabated following his conversion, even in the face of repeated objections from fellow believers.

In 1918, Lewis moved in with Jane Moore, a married woman who was senior to Lewis by twenty-six years and had a young daughter still at home.[280] The extent of this thirty-year relationship remains a mystery to this present day. The details were rarely touched on by Lewis, and even his closest friends have left scant information.

Following the death of Albert Lewis in 1929, his son Warnie became part of Jack and Janie's household, but even his extensive memoirs of the Lewis family leave his brother's personal life, especially concerning Janie, largely untouched. All of this can be troubling to people of faith who are aware that Lewis' conversion transpired about midway through this thirty-year arrangement.

There are obvious moral implications that accompany any discussion of Jack and Janie's affectionate friendship. An accurate assessment is impossible to attain from our vantage point, because key information is simply unavailable. Without the specifics, we are left with speculations, nothing more. In the interest of honesty, Lewis needs to be seen not as

[278] Alan Jacobs, *The Narnian* (New York, NY: HarperCollins, 2005), 1–4.

[279] A.N. Wilson, *C.S. Lewis: A Biography* (London, UK: Harper Perennial, 2005), 259, 263, 265, 281.

[280] Ibid., xvi.

an icon to be revered but as a real flesh and blood human being to be appreciated. In the words of A.N. Wilson, we must determine above all else "to be realistic, not only because reality is more interesting than fantasy, but also because we do Lewis no honour to make him into a plaster saint. And he deserves our honour."[281]

The first brush with religious experience for Jack and Warren Lewis came from their Christian parents who took their boys to an Anglican church in Belfast. They taught their sons how to say their prayers and gave them limited instructions in the Christian faith. But this early acquaintance with Christianity held minimal interest for the young C.S. Lewis.

In his early years, Jack was home-schooled by his mother and governess, Annie Harper, a Presbyterian. From her, Lewis began to see the reality of the eternal state, the other world, representing one small step in his spiritual journey.

In 1905, the Lewis family moved into a new home built by Lewis' father in a suburb of Belfast. This spacious house still stands and is fondly remembered by Albert's famous younger son in his many writings.[282] In this home could be found numerous bookshelves in almost every room.

On the second floor, Jack and Warnie found the now-famous "little end room" with its wardrobe filled with fur coats. It was here that C.S. Lewis' fiery imagination found fertile soil in which to grow and mature the fascinating children's stories which would later make his name famous. It would be many years before these stories, which often portrayed biblical teachings, were published and welcomed by adults and children alike. At least some of the stories found in The Chronicles of Narnia had their genesis in that "little end room." *The Lion, the Witch, and the Wardrobe* comes to mind immediately.

Some writers have argued that Lewis' first religious experience was triggered by the death of his mother on August 23, 1908 when he

[281] Ibid., xviii.

[282] C.S. Lewis, *Surprised by Joy* (London, UK: HarperCollins, 1955), 6–11.

was nine years old. This issue is addressed by Lewis in his spiritual autobiography, *Surprised by Joy*. He tells how he had hoped his mother would be healed of the cancer that claimed her life. Then, following her death, he dared to hope for her restoration to life.

Writing of his mother's passing forty-three years later, he freely admits where he had gone wrong at this most emotionally painful time of his life.

> I had approached God or my idea of God, without love, without awe, even without fear. He was in my mental picture of this miracle, to appear neither as Saviour nor as Judge, but merely as a magician; and when He had done what was required of Him I supposed He would simply-well-go away.[283]

Lewis always felt distanced from his cold and unaffectionate Welsh father, and with his mother gone he became convinced that everything secure, reliable, and meaningful in life had slipped away. At a later time, he found a mother figure in Janie Moore, to whom he often applied the appellation of "mother."

It was in the Wynyard School in Watford, England, the first of several boarding schools attended by Lewis, that for the first time a longing was awakened in him for something more than the usual religious fare. He attended worship services twice each Sunday where he found people who sincerely believed the biblical doctrines the school taught, and he began to pray and read the Bible in a serious manner.

At this juncture, he seemed to have been well on his odyssey of grace and road to joy, but all of this would soon be seen as a false start.[284] Scholars differ as to the depth of faith attained by Lewis at Wynyard and what led to an abandonment of his Christian faith several years later.

At the age of thirteen, he entered Cherbourg school near Malvern, situated near an ancient battlefield in England. By the time he had left

---

[283] Ibid., 21–22.

[284] Ibid., 36–37.

this school in the summer of 1913, he had slipped away from Christian faith into agnosticism, finally plummeting into the abyss of atheism where he would remain for more than fifteen years.

Looking back to his time at Cherbourg forty years later, Lewis spoke approvingly of school matron Miss Cowie, a woman of commendable character but whose subtle influence wreaked havoc on Jack Lewis' fledgling faith. Sewing seeds of doubt on the truths revealed in the Bible at every turn, she charmed her hearers with everything from occultism (including seances and ouija boards), theosophy (meditation), evolution, agnosticism, unitarianism, and a spirituality that would today be called "new age." She rejected divine revelation, replacing it with "higher thought" setting us free from all biblical strictures. As Lewis later described it, "there was nothing to be obeyed, and nothing to be believed."[285]

There were probably other factors at work in the mind of C.S. Lewis, but Miss Cowie's deliberations personified the popular thinking of the age in which she lived.

The odyssey of grace for C.S. Lewis was a long and protracted struggle that lasted until he finally surrendered to the claims of Christ on his life. From his boyhood days in Belfast to the youthful experiences at boarding schools and then into adulthood, he could never escape his longing for purpose and meaning. He enjoyed boisterous laughter, especially with men, but his heart continually ached for peace and joy. The more he tried to dismiss God from his life, the more he was convinced that God did indeed exist and that Jesus Christ the Son of God did walk our planet two thousand years ago.

As Lewis made his way into the halls of Oxford as a lecturer in the 1920s, he became aware that among the professors and students were committed Christians who freely spoke about their faith. As a convinced atheist, Lewis also carried with him a strong anti-Catholicism that he'd inherited from the strong Protestantism in which he'd been raised in Belfast.

[285] Ibid., 66–68.

In 1926, he became acquainted with John Ronald Reuel Tolkien, professor at Oxford, a practicing Roman Catholic and committed Christian. Lewis had been taught that no Catholic could go to heaven and was acquainted with some of the writings of G.K. Chesterton, a Roman Catholic and Christian apologist who defended the truth and accuracy of the Bible. To this day, the works of Chesterton are read and appreciated by many, including evangelical Christians.[286]

By the year of the worldwide financial crash in 1929, Jack Lewis was being unhorsed from his atheistic saddle and the fall would be heard all over the academic world of England and beyond. This was not conversion but a giant leap in his spiritual journey. Lewis describes the moment as he knelt in his Oxford room to acknowledge God:

> You must picture me alone in that room in Magdalen, night after night, feeling, whenever in my mind lifted even for a second from my work, the steady, unrelenting approach of Him whom I so earnestly desired not to meet. That which I greatly feared had at last came upon me. In the Trinity Term of 1929 I gave in, and admitted that God was God, and knelt and prayed: perhaps, that night, the most dejected and reluctant convert in all England. I did not then see what is now the most shining and obvious thing; the Divine humility which will accept a convert even on such terms.[287]

Once Lewis had crossed the threshold from atheism to theism, he returned to the practices he had adopted while at the Wynyard School from 1908–1910. In his later years, he spoke often of his experiences at Wynyard, including harsh discipline from a teacher the boys called Oldie. He had also found the English weather, with its bitter frost, excessive heat, and ongoing fog, to be far harsher than that of Ireland. The school conditions were so difficult that Lewis likened it to a

---

[286] Wilson, *C.S. Lewis: A Biography*, 108.

[287] Lewis, *Surprised by Joy*, 266.

concentration camp, but he reminds us that it was here that he adopted the practice of attending worship services twice each Sunday and heard the teachings of the Bible presented with deep conviction.[288]

Lewis returned to these habits while attending daily chapel at Magdalen College at Oxford. However, he hadn't yet realized that he was also repeating a wrong motivation. Just as at Watford, while at Oxford he was leaning on good works to gain favour with God. He would soon learn that salvation is all of God and all of grace.

In the two years before his conversion, he learned an important lesson he hadn't grasped while at Wynyard as a young boy. In his desperate search for joy, he was exhausting himself with futile efforts to please God and finally came to the end of himself. One author describes it this way:

> He tried with all his might to keep the moral low and inevitably failed. It was, he could see, by the mercy of Christ and his forgiveness alone that he or any of us would be saved, not by our own goodness. He had the cart before the horse: We don't get good before God accepts us; rather, God accepts us, places us under new management, and *then* we begin to have a moral life that comes from the inside out... God's focus is relationship, not religious observance... God is at the center and not we ourselves.[289]

The odyssey of grace for the learned scholar from Oxford was a torturous journey for the first thirty years of his life. Even after his acceptance of the existence of God, Lewis remained stubbornly opposed to acknowledging his need of a Saviour, but the Holy Spirit remained in active pursuit of this wayward son of Adam.

In his heart, Lewis knew he was in a predicament, and like the artful dodger in the Charles Dickens' *Oliver Twist* he did everything in

---

[288] Ibid., 26–27.

[289] Wayne Martindale, *Beyond the Shadowlands* (Wheaton, IL: Crossway Books, 2005), 208–209.

his power to flee from God while attending church and making efforts to be religiously good. Lewis described his emotional ordeal:

> People who are naturally religious find difficulty in understanding the horror of such a revelation. Amiable agnostics will talk cheerfully about "man's search for God." To me, as I was then, they might as well have talked about the mouse's search for the cat.[290]

As Lewis struggled to free himself from what was obviously the convicting work of the Holy Spirit, he could see what he really was by nature. What he later realized is that he was doing everything in his power not to be saved. His rebellious spirit was horrified at the awful picture he now saw for the very first time.

> For the first time, I examined myself with a seriously practical purpose. And there I found what appalled me; a zoo of lusts, a bedlam of ambitious, a nursery of fears, a harem of fondled hatreds. My name was legion.[291]

In the closing pages of *Surprised by Joy*, Lewis describes his agony when he realized that his continued evasion of Christ as God in the flesh was both shameful and futile. The evidence was so great that he could no longer live in such misery and denial. For two years, he held out against what he knew to be true.

For him, it all came together in an instant on September 28, 1931.

> I know very well when, but hardly know-how, the first step was taken. I was driven to Whipsnade one sunny morning. When we set out I did not believe that Jesus Christ is the Son of God, and when we reached the zoo I did. Yet I had not exactly spent

[290] Lewis, *Surprised by Joy*, 265.

[291] Ibid., 263.

> the journey in thought. Nor in great emotion… it was more like when a man, after a long sleep, still lying motionless in bed, becomes aware that he is now awake.[292]

The man who had searched so long in so many places for the meaning of life found it in Jesus Christ.

> When Lewis discovered that his deepest imaginative experiences were linked with what his intellect pushed him to acknowledge—that God in Christ is the creator of all, source of the moral law and guarantor of our eternal home—he was profoundly converted to Christianity, heart and soul, body and mind, to the last fibre of his being. He stopped his vain pursuit of joy as an end in itself, but never stopped writing about it.[293]

During his lifetime, Jack Lewis wore many hats, including that of poet, novelist, academic, essayist, and Christian apologist. He was also a prolific writer churning out dozens of books and periodicals. One of his finest was *Mere Christianity*, a title coined from the words of the seventeenth-century Anglican writer Richard Baxter.[294] This book was instrumental in the conversion of Chuck Colson, who had been President Nixon's most trusted advisor and who spent time in prison for his part in the Watergate scandal.

Hardly anyone took notice when C.S. Lewis passed away on November 22, 1963. Less than an hour after he collapsed and died at home, U.S. President John F. Kennedy was assassinated in Dallas, Texas. Aldous Huxley of *Brave New World* fame also passed on this same day in California, but the passing of both Lewis and Huxley was overshadowed by those events in Texas.

---

[292] Ibid., 275.

[293] Martindale, *Beyond the Shadowlands*, 124.

[294] Jacobs, *The Narnian*, 212–213.

Intellectual honesty had compelled Jack Lewis to recognize that Jesus is exactly who He claimed to be in the New Testament. He was God, come in the flesh, who lived among us and following three years of public ministry offered Himself as the perfect sacrifice for our sins. Faith in Christ means, like Lewis, that we must let go of all defences, confess that we are rebels, and surrender to His mercy and grace. Receiving Christ as our Lord and Saviour enlightens our understanding and brings us to rejoicing and peace, which takes us from here into eternity where we will enjoy His Presence forever.

What Lewis was searching for, and unknown to Him at the time, was a personal relationship with the God he had tried desperately to avoid. Only after God had closed in on him with deep conviction did Lewis freely choose to trust in Christ alone for his salvation.

This somewhat strange dichotomy, God's sovereignty and our responsibility, is beautifully expressed by C.S. Lewis:

> The Prodigal Son at least walked home on his own feet. But who can duly adore that Love which will open the high gates to a prodigal who is brought in kicking, struggling, resentful and darting his eyes in every direction for a chance to escape? The words...compel them to come in, have been so abused by wicked men that we shudder at them; but, properly understood, they plumb the depth of the Divine mercy. The hardness of God is kinder than the softness of men, and His compulsion is our liberation.[295]

The Apostle Peter reminds us, *"Whom having not seem, ye love; in whom, though now ye see him not, yet believing, ye rejoice with joy unspeakable and full of glory: receiving the end of your faith, even the salvation of your souls"* (1 Peter 1:8–9, KJV).

In Hebrews 11:27, the great faith chapter, we are asked to consider the faith of an Old Testament saint, Moses. His faith in God enabled

[295] Lewis, *Surprised by Joy*, 266.

him not to be intimidated by Pharaoh; he was able to persevere because he saw Him who is invisible.

Christianity is all about God and His work of grace on earth. This isn't just another religious system. It is like no other.

These memorable words come from C.S. Lewis, whose odyssey of grace was fraught with so much turmoil: "I believe in Christianity as I believe that the sun has risen—not only because I see it, but because by it, I see everything else."[296]

The long and protracted struggle that culminated in his dramatic conversion was surely a lesson for C.S. Lewis about the measure of God's love. As 1 John 4:19 says, *"We love him because he first loved us"* (ESV). From this verse, we learn that God always takes the initiative, something which was vividly demonstrated for us on the cross (Romans 5:8).

The essence of God's love has been ably caught in the words of the following poem written by Herman Roache (1914–2016), a published poet who was born and raised in West Head, near Lockeport, Nova Scotia:

### LOVE

I was on my way home and the day was far spent
When I noticed a crowd by the way.
I stopped and asked what all of this meant.
They said, "The master is passing this way."
I saw the lame and the blind being lifted up
And sent happily on their way
And I stood amazed at the things I saw done
By the hands of my "Saviour" that day.
A woman who had an issue of blood
And longed for the touch of his hand
Was made every bit whole, both body and soul

[296] Michael Horton, *The Gospel Commission* (Grand Rapids, MI: Baker Books, 2011), 238.

By "God" and my "Saviour's" command.
Times have changed. It's another day.
I'm on that same road again.
Instead of cheers, there is hatred and sneers
For the "man" in the lead is full of pain.
For the cross that he carried was much too big
And his back was bleeding and sore.
And his brow was wet with blood and sweat
From the crown of thorns that he wore.
I was one of the men that stood by that day
And watched his young life diminish
And heard him say in a weakened voice
To his "Father on high", "It is finished!"
I walked away with a heavy heart
But I knew that the job was done.
Somewhere on high, above the sky
He'd greet his "loving son."[297]

---

[297] Herman Roache, "Love." Permission granted by Roache's family.

OUR GREATEST TREASURE

**Is the Bible a trustworthy document, or is it filled with errors and** contradictions as claimed by the skeptics? In *Our Greatest Treasure*, we examine the evidence.

Less than two centuries ago, many scholars argued convincingly that the Hittites never existed, even though they are mentioned in the Bible more than fifty times. The unearthing of their massive library in Turkey has revealed an advanced civilization that once rivalled both Egypt and Assyria. Not many years ago, Ahab's house of ivory was considered impossible, but not now. His wife, Jezebel, was dismissed as a fictional character inserted into the text to arouse interest, but the recent discovery of her signet ring with her name clearly discernible has silenced the critics. At one time, historians were convinced that Gallio in Acts 18 never existed, but the spade of the archaeologists has uncovered his name, his position as Proconsul of Achaia, and even the time of his service in Corinth.

Men and women from both distant times and the present have had their lives transformed by the message of the Bible. Many of the people, places, and events found in the Bible are found in no other literature, and their details have been documented as being authentic by historical and archaeological research. The Bible is not buried treasure. It is open to all who will access its sacred pages. The Bible is indeed *Our Greatest Treasure*.

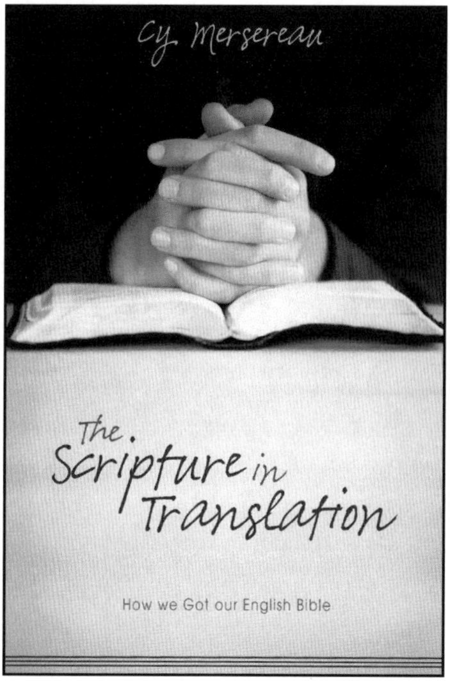


SCRIPTURE IN TRANSLATION

**Contrary to popular assumption, the large proliferation of varied** English versions of the Bible is not a recent phenomenon; it can be traced back to a much earlier time, long before the King James Version came on the scene. But with so many versions of the Bible available today, how do we determine which one is best for us? Is the argument for only one version in the English language actually valid, and should that one version be the KJV?

*Scripture in Translation* begins with the account of how the Bible was extracted from ancient languages into English, only to face violent opposition on the shores of England itself. The journey continues with dramatic historical events that impacted Bible translation and publishing—such as the fourteenth-century translator who was taken to court and condemned by the church of the day (decades *after* his death!)—and finishes by looking at the strengths and weaknesses of the editions available to us today.

UNTIL SHILOH COMES

**It is incredible that the first promise of a coming Messiah came not** to our first parents, Adam and Eve, but to the serpent who had so deceitfully engineered their downfall. Genesis 3:15 records that God's promised Seed of the woman was destined to defeat the seed of the serpent, which anticipated the gospel of the Lord Jesus Christ. This is known as the "first good news," or *proto evangel um*, whose blessed promise became the focal point of the entire Old Testament.

Threading its way through Abraham and his descendants, this promise came to rest on his great grandson, Judah, and remained there for all succeeding generations, finding fruition in the first coming of the Messiah, indicated by the words of Genesis 49:10, "until Shiloh comes." Throughout history, Bible scholars have largely agreed that Shiloh, which means peace, references the first coming of the Lord Jesus Christ, the Prince of Peace, the Lion of the tribe of Judah.

The Old Testament is the foundational document for all that follows in the New Testament and should never be relegated to inferior status. These older scriptures were given for our admonition and should be esteemed and appreciated in the same manner as the New Testament writings until Shiloh comes, the second time.